A COMPLETE HOW-TO MANUAL BY MICHAEL GÄRTNER

GINGKO PRESS

CONTENTS

FOREWORD

Boris Gärtner polishes the edge of a new leather sole, Kallhäll shoemaker's shop, 1957.

My name is Michael Gärtner, and I grew up with a father who was one of Sweden's best shoemakers in the 1950s and '60s. During the '50s, Dad was an apprentice for Erik Andersson in Stockholm. Erik was a talented and famous fifth-generation shoemaker who was often hired by the major newspapers for articles about shoe care, among other things. Erik's shoemaker's shop on the hill of Hantverkargatan (handworker's street) still exists today and was operated by the family up until a few years ago. After his apprenticeship with a diploma from the Master Shoemakers' Guild, my father opened his own shoemaker's shop in Kallhäll, north of Stockholm.

As a little boy, I found the shoemaking workshop to be an exciting place, with tools and machines, knives, punches and cutting machines. But it was not exactly a suitable play area, so more often than not, I was relegated to less dangerous tasks, like searching in bags full of leather remnants. There, at an early age, I could explore leather's different characteristics and detect differences in the quality of flimsy belly leather and stiff back leather. When Dad had the time, he would help me make something exciting, like a cowboy holster or a quiver that I longed for. *Bonanza* and *The High Chaparral* were on television at that time – Buck and Manolito were big idols. Was I held in high regard among my friends when I came out to play with a "real" cowboy holster? You bet!

After receiving several diplomas and winning competitions in the art of shoemaking, my father was offered a job in the United States. The whole family ended up in Charlotte, North Carolina, where my father won the Shoe Service Institute of America's National Silver Cup in 1968, a world prize arguably the highest in the shoemaking industry. After the SSIA prize, the shoemaking business was booming and Dad needed help to prepare shoes needing repair. I accompanied my father to the shoemaker's shop on Saturdays and holidays. Not so much fun for a boy in his early teens, but rubber heels and nails needed to be removed and leather soles gently loosened. It took some time before I was of real use but, at 15, I did almost all the preparatory work. Dad took care of the final finishing.

In 1974, life took a new turn and we were back again in Jakobsberg, north of Stockholm. I was very interested in music, and if I wanted to listen to my favorites – the Eagles, Pink Floyd and Led Zeppelin – I had to come up with 35 Swedish crowns (about 4 U.S. dollars) for an LP. Today's radio programming did not exist. Sweden's Radio P3 had a two-hour popular music program with Kaj Kindvall, and that was it. Now, the skills I had learned at my father's shoemaking shop came in handy. My musical interest was funded by the money I earned myself at the shoemaker's in Jakobsberg. I worked there afternoons, after my classes at the high school, doing almost everything that is done in shoemaking and then some. I mended shoes, punched heels and soles and made wooden shoes and belts to sell.

Since the 1960s, quality-made shoes in the shops have gradually been replaced with shoes of inferior quality. The ordinary consumer's quality awareness is low today, and few have their shoes repaired because it is not considered worthwhile. Throwaway consumerism has become so commonplace that we often overpay for rubbish shoes end up in the garbage after just one season.

I hope and believe that this view is beginning to change. Increasingly, more people are breaking with the throwaway trend and buying quality that lasts longer. A pair of good quality shoes today start at more than two hundred dollars. They have genuine leather top sides and insoles as well as outer soles, and heels in leather with rubber treads. The shoes have a lifetime of dozens of years if they are properly cared for, and are an environmentally friendly alternative to throwaway shoes.

Although today I no longer work with shoes, I carry with me a lot of what my father taught me and, among other things, his eye for quality and his accuracy. I have no saddle-making education, nor am I a certified shoemaker or cobbler – I am self-taught. Making things with my own hands has been a strong driving force for me, and my hope is that this book will inspire good craftsmanship. Leatherworking is an inspiring art limited only by your imagination. Taking your time, enjoying the process, and working carefully are the keys to a satisfying and successful result. The feeling of designing, making templates and cutting and sewing your own wallet (for example) is priceless! Good luck!

– MICHAEL GÄRTNER

Shoe Service Institute of America Silver Cup Issue in 1968.

INTRODUCTION

This book is intended to give you basic knowledge about leather and leather handicraft. It is divided into four parts: leather, technique, braiding and projects. In part one, leather is presented as a material; here, you will learn about the tanning process, the different characteristics of finished tanned leather and what you should know before you buy your first hide. Part two begins with an overview of most of the tools used in simple handcrafting with leather. It also describes techniques such as cutting, hole punching, gluing and saddle stitching. Each technique also describes which tools are needed and how to use them. Part three presents braiding and its many uses and includes step-by-step instructions for making several simple flat and round braids as well as certain knots and buttons. In the last part of the book, part four, you can apply your knowledge by completing any of a number of projects, presented from the easiest to the hardest. These projects are only suggestions; it's up to you and your creativity to determine how you complete each project.

Part One
LEATHER

A material that we have used for thousands of years, leather is prized for its natural feel, strength and ability to age with a beautiful patina. It has been copied and plagiarized, but never replaced. In part one, I give you a brief summary of what happens when animal hides from the slaughterhouse get turned into finished leather, and what you need to know before you buy your first piece of leather.

»—→ TANNING

Leather is made from animal hides, most of which are by-products or leftovers from the meat industry, including hides from cow, calf, bull, horse, lamb, deer, kangaroo, goat, pig, and ostrich. Instead of ending up in landfills, tanned hides are used for a variety of objects. The type of leather the finished hide will be is determined by how it is tanned – a cowhide for example, could be a soft leather for furniture or a more stable leather that is well suited to the projects in this book.

It is believed that, before the Bronze Age, the fat and brain matter of killed animals were used for tanning hides, just as Native Americans traditionally treated their deerskin. Leather was also preserved as the Eskimos do today, with urine. Tanning with plant extracts came later and can be traced to the ancient river cultures that existed 8,000–10,000 years ago. How humankind discovered the preservative effects of plants is not certain. One theory is that early humans noticed the difference in animal skins that were left out in puddles and autumn leaves for a long time. Decay was delayed in these hides, unlike those that had not come in contact with wet leaves and bark.

Throughout the centuries, various tannins from plants have been used to preserve and tan hides. Oak bark combined with salt was a common practice, but it could take up to a year for the tanning process to be complete. Until the mid-1800s, this and similar methods with vegetable extracts were used for tanning, but the process took a long time, so other alternatives were sought to shorten the process. In the late 1800s, chromium salts, chromium 3 and chromium 6, were discovered, which shortened the process from several months to a few days.

In the early 1900s, chrome tanning of leather became an industry, and chrome-tanned leather replaced the more expensive vegetable-tanned leather during the latter part of the 1900s. Chrome-tanned leather can be recognized by the underside's bluish color. It is also called "wet blue." Chrome-tanned leather is used for, among other things, footwear, clothing and furniture, and it currently accounts for about 90 percent of all manufactured leather. The tanning industry depends on this method largely for its economic advantages, but from a broader perspective, the benefits are not so obvious. Chromium is environmentally harmful, and therefore only chromium 3 can be used for tanning, and chromium 6 is completely banned throughout the world. There are also safety implications for workers in the tanneries in the low-income countries that supply the Western world with much of its leather. For the consumer, chrome-tanned leather can cause allergies and eczema. Another drawback is that chrome-tanned leather contains heavy metals and thus is not biodegradable. In the long run, this leads to heavy metal waste and disposal problems when products made with chrome-tanned leather, such as cheap shoes, end up in landfills.

In my work, I have chosen to use only vegetable-tanned leather. For me, the choice is simple and obvious. Apart from all the negative aspects of chrome-tanned leather, vegetable-tanned leather has many advantages: It has a real leather scent; when it is soaked, it is easy to shape around a template and then holds its shape when it has dried; and it gets a nice patina with a dark honey-brown color over time.

The plant extract used in tanning leather gives a bright, natural color that varies depending on the composition of the extract. The amount of fat in the skin and the skin's original color also affects how the leather ages and the patina it develops. The natural-colored leather can also be dyed any color in smaller pieces, which is cheaper than buying large hides of dyed leather. You can tan leather so that it is not affected by sunlight and retains its bright color under use. However, many people appreciate leather that ages with a nice patina and a beautiful, dark-brown color.

Depending on the plant extract composition, tanning may also affect the leather's density and flexibility as well as how easy it is to cut. It is best, if you have the opportunity, to visit the tannery yourself so you can choose the best leather for your project. If you buy leather directly from a tannery, you may want to ask about the leather's characteristics. Be sure to ask about how the leather ages so you do not waste time, money and effort on a project that will not maintain the desired characteristics after use.

Vegetable tanning is still a slow process. There are two common methods. One method involves dipping the hides into a series of large vats that have increasingly strong tanning fluid. This method takes several months. In the second method, large barrels are used in which the leather is "tumbled." This method is faster, and today it takes only about a week from hide to finished product. Leather tanned in drums can be easily damaged, but it will be softer and fuller. Each tannery has its own secret "recipe" of various plant extracts that is the result of many generations of experience and knowledge.

The number of tanneries currently producing vegetable-tanned leather from their own traditional recipes is on the wane. In Sweden, for instance, there are only three remaining. Leatherworking done at the hobbyist level cannot secure a leather worker's future, but I want to emphasize the importance of supporting our tanneries. They stand for tradition, craftsmanship, skill and generations of experience.

TANNING STEP BY STEP

When the hides reach the tannery, a week of work begins in order to turn them into finished leather. In total, there are 25 different treatments, described here briefly (not that you need to remember this, but I have chosen to include the various steps of tanning to show its complexity). Small differences in the tanning process allow each tannery to have its own brand.

SALTING Occurs immediately after slaughter and before the hides reach the tannery; involves salting, drying, or freezing hides.

CLEANING Washing the hides.

SOAKING Soaking the hides.

LIMING Removing the hair with the help of sodium chloride as the hide swells.

FACTS

Here is a list of some of the tree extracts used and what effect they give to the natural-colored leather as it ages.

OAK Provides a drab, firm but supple leather.

CHESTNUT Often used in Europe and provides a solid leather with a medium-brown tone.

MIMOSA Comes from the bark of the South African mimosa tree. Common in the United States where it is used with quebracho to produce a leather with a reddish tone that darkens when exposed to light.

QUEBRACHO Extract from a South American tree that gives a full-bodied but slightly "spongy" leather with a reddish tone.

FIR Used primarily in Central Europe and gives a reddish tone to the leather.

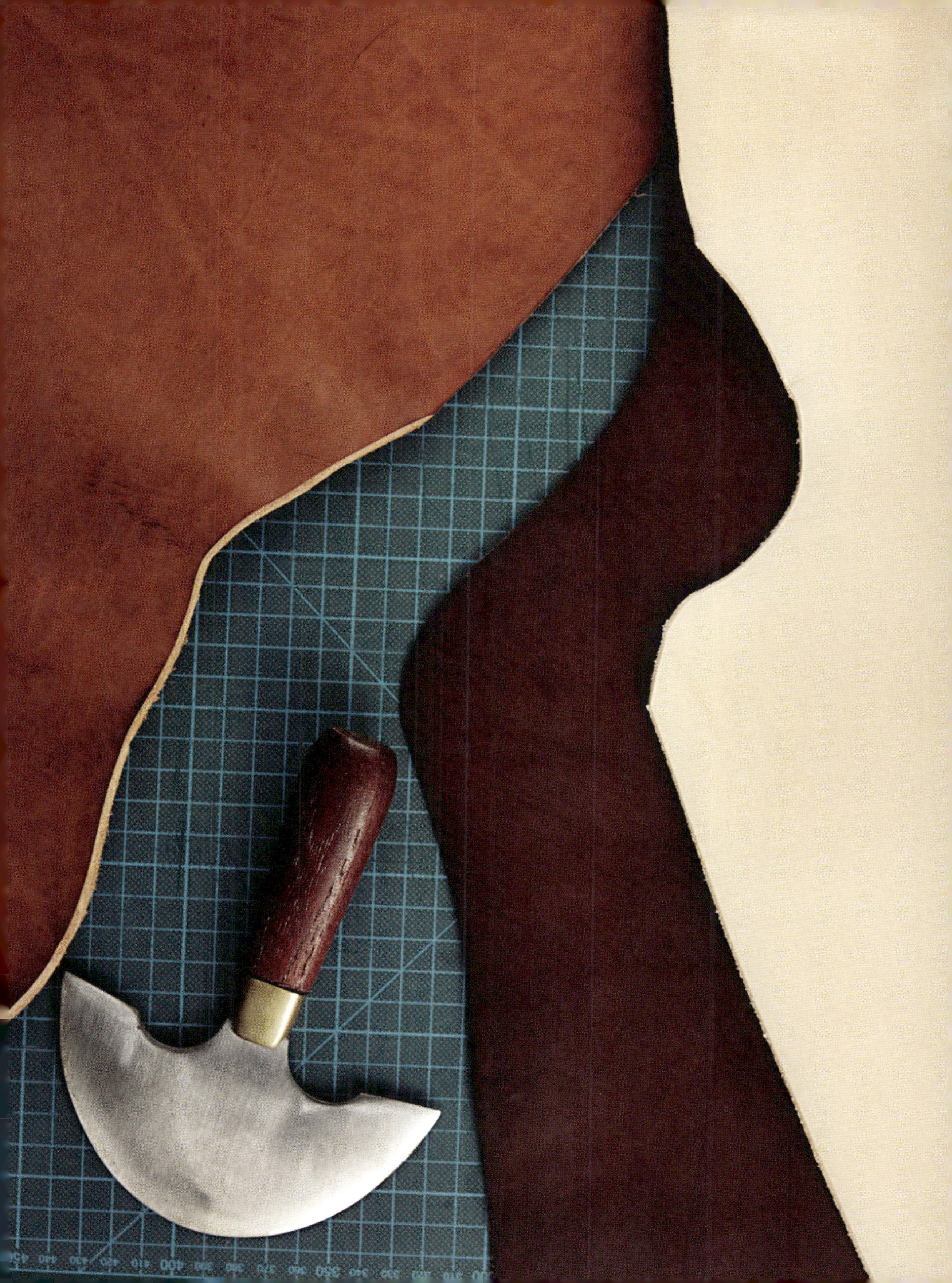

FLESHING Scraping off membranes and meat scraps while simultaneously trimming and batch labeling the hides.

SPLITTING Rough adjustment of the final thickness made by splitting the skin into two layers, the epidermis (hair side) and subcutaneous (flesh side).

DELIMING Removes lime residue.

PICKLING Alkaline neutralization (in preparation for tanning).

PRE-TANNING Further preparation for tanning.

TANNING Preserves the hide.

PRESSING Removes the water and flattens the hide.

FOLDING Fine-tunes the finished dimensions.

BLEACHING Removes iron stains and whitens the hide.

NEUTRALIZATION Raises the pH-balance to allow the fats to penetrate.

AFTER-TANNING Fills loose parts in the hide.

FATLIQUORING Restores fats and oils to the hide.

FIXING Lowers the pH to bind the oils.

SETTING OUT The hides are laid out, and the wrinkles and creases are smoothed out as the water is pressed out.

DRYING The leather is hung or nailed up and dried halfway.

CONDITIONING The leather is smoothed out for final drying.

FINAL DRYING The leather is dried to about 15–18% moisture content.

VACUUM PRESS Used to stretch the leather to restore the surface and reduce stretchability in the finished product.

TRIMMING Hides are trimmed and sorted according to quality.

FINISH To improve the leather's appearance and to protect the leather during use.

MEASUREMENT Measuring the surface of the hides, usually in square feet or square decimeters.

»——→ HIDE

In simplified form, a hide is comprised of a top side (or hair side) which is where the hair is located, and a bottom side called the flesh side. To get more out of the hide, a tannery can divide or split the skin during the tanning process. To do this, the bottom side of the hide is sliced off, so the tannery gets double the surface of the hide. The bottom side that has been split can be used for things such as tool belts, for example, where the quality is not so important. For the projects in the book, only quality leather with the top grain side is used.

»——→ DYEING

The types of dyes and finishes that can be applied at the tannery are aniline dyes, semi-aniline dyes and pigmented coating. It might be good to know these terms when you buy your first hide.

ANILINE DYE A clear dye that allows the leather to retains its natural surface. It can breathe and age over time and has a soft and lovely leather feel. The surface of the leather is not as durable, as it is not a surface treatment.

SEMI-ANILINE DYE Similar to aniline dye, but the leather gets a more durable surface through a light finish.

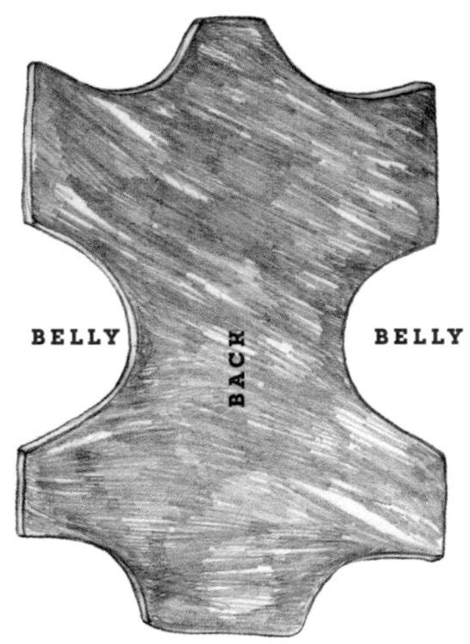

PIGMENTED COATING An exterior finish that is more durable. The drawback is that the leather loses a lot of its soft leather feeling. Blemishes like scars from bites and sores can be hidden with a topcoat.

»——› THE PARTS OF THE TANNED HIDE

Animal hides are divided into three parts: back, neck and belly leather. Back leather, also called croupon, comes from the back portion and the butt of the hide and has a smooth and steady structure. The fibers in back leather are smaller and sit closer together. Collagen in the skin forms these fibrous structures; the denser the fiber structure, the stronger and more stable the leather. Neck and belly leather have a sparse fiber structure and therefore do not have the same stability and durability. On the leather's flesh side, these differences are more apparent than on the hair side. The less stable parts, the neck and belly, have a more "stringy" appearance – the tiny fibers that make up the leather are larger and look sparser. If you scrape it with a fingernail, it is easy to roughen up the flesh side of neck and belly leather. With the finer back leather, on the other hand, the flesh side is considerably firmer and not as easy to roughen up. Back leather does not have the same "stringy" appearance. All of these differences can be seen most after use; the lower quality neck and belly parts stretch and lose shape more easily, and folds can also be seen more clearly than in the firmer back leather. The hide has different characteristics depending on where it is on the animal and how it must adapt to the needs of the animal. The animal needs to have more flexible skin around the throat, neck and belly, but that's less true for the back and butt.

Finished tanned leather is sold as half hides, or sides, where the skin has been divided along the spine, but it can also be sold in portions smaller than whole sides. Since the quality of the leather varies across the hide, different parts are suitable for different leather products. Back leather is suitable for belts and straps because a steady, durable leather that does not stretch is required. The lower-quality, often flabby belly and neck leather can be used in masks and sculpted works of art that are not subject to strain. In some projects, you may even be required to glue flesh side to flesh side to create a more stable piece of leather that also displays the beautiful grain on both sides.

⤜→ THICKNESS

A hide's thickness is usually specified in ounces and varies a few tenths of a millimeter across the hide. As an example, 4 ounces corresponds approximately to the thickness of a quater: 1.6 mm. The thickness of a standard belt is about 7–8 ounces, or about 3 mm. In the shoe business, leather thickness is measured in irons.

It may be best to let the tannery split your hide if your work requires a precise thickness. Tanneries have machines that can split full hides. Smaller pieces can be made in hand-cranked splitting machines; used ones can be found for sale online. A famous brand of splitting machine is the American-made Landis Leather Splitter.

⤜→ LEATHER TYPES

In your work with leather, you will encounter a variety of new concepts, ranging from signs of quality and the names of different parts of the hide to after-tanning treatments and terms that describe the leather from specific animals. Here are some of the most common terms that you will encounter at various retailers.

CORDOVAN Special-tanned back leather from a horse. Because of its ability to withstand water and its durability, cordovan is often used in high-quality men's shoes. Today, the renowned Chicago-based tannery Horween Leather Company more or less has a monopoly on cordovan leather. The leather has become popular among hobbyist leather workers, but it is difficult to buy in smaller quantities because Horween only sells in large quantities.

FULL-GRAIN LEATHER The hair side of full-grain leather is not sanded or otherwise treated to hide any scars or other marks on the hide – it remains in its original state, providing a durable surface to "breathe" and eventually developing a nice patina. Full-grain leather is used in fine shoes and furniture. Only the best hides are used for full-grain leather.

CHROME-TANNED LEATHER This is leather that has been tanned with chromium salts. The leather is water-repellent and therefore is not suitable for dyeing with water-based paints at home. Dyeing is done instead at the tannery, where a variety of colors can be developed. The leather is recognizable by its blue-gray color, unless it is completely color-dyed.

SUEDE Suede is taken from the flesh side of full-grain leather and is abraded or brushed to present a velvety surface. It's

LEATHER THICKNESS

OUNCE	MILLIMETER	IRON	FRACTIONAL INCH	DECIMAL INCH
1	0.4	0.75	1/64	0.016
2	0.8	1.5	1/32	0.031
3	1.2	2.25	3/64	0.047
4	1.6	3	1/16	0.063
5	2	2.75	5/64	0.078
6	2.4	4.5	3/32	0.094
7	2.8	5.25	7/64	0.109
8	3.2	6	1/8	0.125
9	3.6	6.75	9/64	0.141
10	4	7.5	5/32	0.156
11	4.4	8.25	11/64	0.172
12	4.8	9	3/16	0.188

"THE NICE SHINY SIDE OF LEATHER WHERE THE HAIR WAS IS CALLED THE HAIR SIDE."

usually used as the exterior of leather products. A thicker side of full-grain leather can yield several sides of suede leather by splitting it into thinner layers and then brushing them.

NAPA This term usually refers to aniline-dyed calfskin, sheepskin or goatskin. Napa is very soft and is used in products such as finer clothing items, purses and toiletry bags.

NUBUCK Nubuck is aniline-dyed leather that has been sanded or buffed on the grain side. Nubuck is sensitive to dirt and is hard to clean.

ELK AND DEER LEATHER These types of leather are durable and prized by indigenous peoples such as various American Indian tribes. This leather no longer comes from wild animals but rather from the hides of animals in captivity. It's used to make jackets, coats and gloves.

KANGAROO LEATHER Kangaroo is a durable, soft leather used in braiding in items such as whips, motorcycle clothing and expensive soccer shoes.

OSTRICH LEATHER Ostrich leather is considered very high quality and durable. Today, it is used in fashion accessories of well-known, expensive brands. Ostrich leather has a characteristic goose flesh surface as a result of the follicles where the feathers were.

RAWHIDE Rawhide is an untanned hide that is scraped, soaked and treated with lime to become stiff and brittle. Rawhide is used for chew toys for dogs, drum heads and the finer braiding for the detailed work in leather products, such as whips.

SPLIT LEATHER This is the bottom layer of a hide. Split leather is sliced from the finer top side, or top grain, during the tanning process.

Split leather is used for a variety of leather products that do not need a fine grain, such as tool belts. Split leather can be stained and finished to resemble the finer top grain and is used to make cheaper shoes. Coated, split leather can be recognized by its dense, unnatural and plastic-like top side.

VEGETABLE-TANNED LEATHER This is leather that has been tanned with different extracts from bark, leaves, trees or other plant parts.

Part two

TECHNIQUE & DESIGN

In part two I go through the tools, how to join pieces of leather with gluing or sewing, how to make patterns plus some other useful information. In the Tools Overview section you will find a brief description of most of the tools required for handcrafted leather work; how to use each tool is described in the sections that follow. In the projects described in part four, I often refer to the techniques described in this section. For that reason, it's a good idea to take the time to read through part two and even practice the different steps before moving on to the projects – better to try saddle stitching for the first time on a spare piece of leather than on any of your projects.

TOOLS OVERVIEW

Good tools will simplify your work and make the final result look professional, but look at your leatherworking endeavors as an investment over time. The number and quality of tools you choose to buy is a matter of your taste and finances. Search online first; a lower-quality version of a tool that costs a small amount at your local craft store can cost ten times as much if you choose the most expensive and finest quality. On page 125, you will find a list of dealers. An option for the beginner is one of the leatherworking tool kits that are sold on the internet (eBay and Amazon). Many are made in China and are not of the highest quality, but the price is usually affordable.

1. BEESWAX Used to wax and make cotton thread stronger. It can also be used to wax the pricking iron to make perforation easier or for the finishing touch for edge buffing.

2. DAFA ROTARY CUTTER My favorite knife, ideal for making straight cuts using a ruler – the leather will remain in place under the ruler, unlike when using other straight blade knives.

3. CRAFT KNIFE Used for cutting patterns or round shapes in leather. Another option is an X-Acto or hobby knife with replaceable blades. The No. 1 and No. 2 sizes are suitable for cutting.

4. PRICKING IRON Used to make seam perforations for saddle stitching. Pricking irons are available with a different number of points and with various distances between the points.

5. GLASS SLICKER A piece of glass that is one centimeter thick and has been ground so it's round and smooth around the edges. A glass slicker is used primarily to shape wet leather. It can also be used to press pieces of leather together after gluing.

6. END PUNCH Used to cut off the ends of straps and belts. Available in U-shaped or English point versions, as well as in a variation with rounded corners (not pictured).

7. SLAB A surface for using various punching tools (not pictured).

8. PUNCH Available in round and oblong or oval, and in different sizes. The round punch can be used to make holes in belts and to fasten rivets and snaps. The oval punch can be used to make holes to fasten straps.

9. BURNISHER A hand tool made of nylon or hardwood. The wooden burnisher creates greater friction and polishes the leather faster. There are also small cocobolo wood burnishing tips that fit the Dremel tool and make the job even easier. Many saddle makers also use a rough, white canvas cloth for burnishing since the rough fabric provides good friction.

10. EDGER OR BEVELER Smoothes the edges of leather. Available with straight or round cutting edges and in various widths – 1–3 mm works for simpler jobs. The edger must be well-honed and sharp in order to do a good job.

11. CONTACT CEMENT OR ADHESIVE Used to glue two pieces of leather before they are sewn together. Available in both water-based and solvent-based types.

12. RULER Having rules of two different lengths – 30 cm and 100 cm – is a must. It also helps to have a thick ruler, about 2 mm, that weighs enough to keep the leather in place when cutting (not pictured).

13. LEATHER CONDITIONER OR LEATHER GREASE Softens and conditions the leather, available in many different varieties and brands.

20
13
SPORT
OURALINE
DEPUIS 1822
PROTECTION EAU PLUIE NEIGE BOUE
GRAISSE DUBBIN
Saphir
IMPERMEABILISE
4
9
15
1
28
OFF
ON
ZERO
inch/mm
26
STAINLESS
HARDENED
5
23
22

3
29
31
2
11
ECOWELD™
WATER BASED CONTACT CEMENT
CEMENT DE CONTACTO DEL AQUA BASADA
ADHÉSIF DE CONTACT À BASE D'EAU
Tandy Leather Factory
MANUFACTURED IN ITALY
16.9 fl oz • 500 ml e
17
トコノール
無色
18
14
27

14. LEATHER SHEARS Heavier than scissors that are used for paper or fabric, and with a serrated edge so that they don't slip when cutting thicker leather.

15. SADDLE MAKER'S SCRATCH COMPASS OR GAUGE COMPASS To make it easy to get a straight seam, use a compass to mark where you are going to make holes for the seam with your pricking iron.

16. PENCIL COMPASS Used to draw patterns and shapes (not pictured).

17. BURNISHING COMPOUND OR GUM TRAGACANTH Used to polish the edges of the leather. Tragacanth is a gum-like substance from the resin of certain bushes.

18. ROLLER Used to press two pieces of leather together after gluing.

19. BLUNT AWL OR FID Used to tighten or widen the distance between the strands in a braid. The awl has a blunt tip and rounded edges to prevent damage to the leather when it is inserted between the strands.

20. STRAP CUTTER OR DRAW GAUGE Has an adjustable blade for cutting leather straps.

21. REVOLVING OR ROTARY PUNCH A punch with a rotary head and punch tubes of varying sizes, 1–6 mm (not shown).

22. RUBBER OR GUM ERASER Used to remove adhesive residue or wax pen marks.

23. RAWHIDE HAMMER OR MALLET Made of rawhide or plastic, both types of mallets work well and will not harm other tools (do not use a steel or an iron hammer, which can damage punches and the like).

24. CREASING IRON OR SCREW CREASE For adjustable marking of a line along the edge of the leather for sewing or decoration, such as along the edge of a belt.

25. WOODEN CREASER Same as a creasing iron but the creaser is not adjustable. It usually has four fixed widths to mark a line along the edge of the leather (not pictured).

26. HARNESS NEEDLE A needle with a rounded tip that comes in various sizes. The needle lacks a sharp tip because a pricking iron or diamond-shaped awl make the holes for saddle stitching.

27. STITCHING PONY Keeps your work in place so you can use both hands for sewing.

28. CALIPER OR SLIDE RULE Used for precise measuring and marking patterns directly onto the leather.

29. SKIVER Planes or slices leather down to the desired thickness, for example after joining or gluing two pieces of leather.

30. CUTTING MAT A surface for cutting leather (not shown).

31. STANLEY KNIFE BLADE Used for cutting leather. The loose blade from a Stanley knife can be used along with a rawhide mallet or hammer to "punch" out straight cuts in the leather.

32. AWL Available in two types: round or diamond-shaped. An awl with a diamond-shaped tip is used to make the seam holes for saddle stitching when you are not using a pricking iron. An awl with a round tip is used to repair old seams so the thread is not damaged when it is inserted. I also use the round awl to make marks for patterns or for hole punching.

10
33
24
19
32
32
8
6
6
8
8
C.S OSBORNE MADE IN U.S.A.

33. STITCHING GROOVER Used to cut a groove in the leather to mark where the saddle stitch will be placed. The seam is recessed into the groove, which helps protect the stitching.

34. THREAD Made of synthetic or linen fibers. Linen has a natural feel but is not as long-lasting. Synthetic lasts longer and you can easily secure it by melting the end of the thread.

35. WAX PEN For marking on leather. Easy to remove with a rubber eraser (not pictured).

»——→ CUTTING WITH PATTERNS

In the leather industry, large punching machines and punching dies made of iron that's 2 mm thick are used for cutting patterns in leather. Iron dies have a precise shape for each piece of leather; for example, a pair of shoes has its own dies, and all the details are in the cutting tool. Large pieces of leather are placed in the machine and the iron dies are then placed on top. The lever is pressed with a two-handed grip so that no fingers can get caught in between, and precise pieces of leather are punched out. Using this method, the shoe industry cuts out leather and no extra work or additional trimming is needed.

If you don't have access to an expensive punch and dies, you can make patterns out of cardboard and cut out the leather by hand. If you choose to work without patterns, with every new project, you will need to measure and mark where to cut, put rivets and so on. This means that your credit card case or cell phone case may look a little different each time.

When I get an idea for a new project, I start by sketching on a blank piece of graph paper using a ruler and a compass. I use the compass to draw circular shapes and corners, but you can also use finished stencils of circles and round corners of various sizes, which can be found at office supply stores. Use a pencil with a fine point, because when you go to cut out the pattern with a straight blade, it is easier to follow a narrow line than a wide one. You want the finished pattern to be as accurate as possible. It is also important to think about how you will assemble your project. For a cell phone case with an extra pocket for a credit card, the leather must be cut slightly wider than a case without an extra pocket. An extra pocket requires an extra layer of leather, which makes the case thicker, and therefore the front and back need to be wider. It often takes a few tries before you get it right – cutting for form and function requires some thought.

After drawing the different parts, it's time to clip or cut them out. I usually use a ruler and a rotary cutter for the straight

TIPS!

Symmetrical patterns are easiest to draw on the right or left half of a piece of graph paper, then fold the pattern on the center line and trace the pattern on the opposite side.

parts and a small craft knife for round shapes. I make sure to cut in the middle of the pencil line.

When you have cut out all the pieces of paper, glue them to a thick piece of cardboard, preferably not any thicker than 1 mm because then it becomes difficult to cut. The cardboard must withstand glue without losing its shape and becoming wavy. It needs to be sturdy since you will use the patterns many times. Apply glue to the pieces of paper and be sure to spread the glue evenly out to the edges. Firmly press the pieces of paper with glue to the cardboard. Smooth out any wrinkles. If necessary, you can press the cardboard flat under some books with plastic film in between.

When the glue has dried, it is time to once again use the ruler, rotary cutter and craft knife to cut out the patterns. The more precisely you manage to cut your patterns, the less work and fixing you need to do afterward. Now you have patterns that you can use again and again to mark and cut out the leather for your projects. Place the pattern or patterns on the leather and mark carefully around the pattern with an awl on the leather's hair side. The mark from the awl should only just be visible, and should not go through the surface of the leather's hair side. If you have a full side of leather, you should consider which areas of the leather to use for the different parts of your project. The parts of the leather that sit along the spine and butt are of sturdier quality than those parts around the belly and neck. Plan your cutting and use the weaker parts of the leather for the less important pieces.

To make even simple things like a belt, I use patterns to set the width of my strap cutter (see next page). On the same pattern, I have also marked the holes I need to make in the belt so that they are centered and evenly spaced.

»—→ CUTTING TOOLS

LARGE CUTTING MAT Using a cutting mat as a base is a must to protect your knives and the table you are working on. A cutting mat that is approximately 60 cm × 100 cm is suitable for that. If you need a larger cutting surface, you can move the mat, provided the table underneath is large enough. A leather hide can be up to 200 cm long and for that a larger table is helpful.

LONG AND SHORT RULER I have two rulers: one that is 100 cm and a shorter one that is 30 cm. I use the longer one almost exclusively for when I need to cut large pieces of leather. The shorter ruler is handy and perfect to use for all projects. Rulers with some weight to them are a plus because they can help hold the leather in place better while cutting.

KNIVES There are a variety of knives for leather working. A more expensive, quality knife for cutting contours is L'Indispensable Knife from the French manufacturer Vergez Blanchard (pictured on page 19). It has a blade that can be resharpened and is replaceable. This knife's blade is slightly stronger than that of craft knives, so the tip doesn't break as easily. The downside is that this knife requires care and knowledge to maintain a sharp edge. The cheaper straight blades (see below) cannot be resharpened.

ROTARY CUTTER For longer cuts along the edge of a ruler, I prefer to use a Dafa brand rotary cutter, available in regular craft stores. Rotary blades are perfect for cutting along the edge of a ruler because they do not move the leather as a standard straight knife does. Even if you push the ruler hard against the leather, it can shift and you can end up cutting it wrong. A rotary cutter therefore operates better when you are making long, straight cuts.

STRAIGHT BLADE KNIVES Small, cheap, straight blades of hobby craft quality are available in different sizes and can do the job if you need to cut round or other types of shapes in leather. Remember to keep the knife at a 90-degree angle to the leather. This is especially important when cutting around corners where it is easy to tilt the knife. If you get a cut that is not angled 90 degrees to the leather, the parts will not fit together. It takes practice to cut round shapes with a hobby knife. Small mistakes can be fixed later by sanding with sandpaper.

CIRCLE COMPASS LEATHER CUTTER

For several of the projects in the book, I have chosen to make round buttons out of leather. Cutting round pieces with a knife is difficult, but with this Japanese tool it becomes much easier. The tool is a compass with a replaceable razor blade that cuts out perfectly round pieces from 1.8 cm to about 10 cm in diameter. This tool is not listed in any of the projects, but it can be useful. It is available for purchase at GoodsJapan.jp.

LEATHER SHEARS As described earlier, leather shears are more powerful than scissors used to cut paper or fabric. They have serrated edges so that thicker leather cannot slide between the blades.

STANLEY KNIFE BLADES Another knife blade that I use to make shorter straight cuts is a replaceable blade for a Stanley knife. The blade is about 10 cm long and can be broken into shorter lengths. You can use the blade's edge as a punch tool. If, for example, you want to make a magic braid and want three equally wide parts for the braid, use the Stanley knife blade by placing the sharp edge against the leather and then gently tapping the back of the blade with a rawhide mallet or hammer.

This straight blade can also be used to cut rounded corners: Select first where to cut, then put the sharp edge on the marking and tap with a rawhide mallet. If you do this repeatedly, gradually moving the blade a few millimeters forward each time and working your way around the marking, you get an almost round corner. The corner is more rounded the less distance you move the blade between each cut. For a final rounding touch, rub with sandpaper or a nail file. The advantage of using this method is that it is easier to cut at a 90-degree angle to the leather's surface.

STRAP CUTTER OR DRAW GAUGE

This is an invaluable tool if you want to cut straight, smooth straps. The strap cutter can be set to the desired width up to 100 mm and is capable of cutting leather up to 6 mm in thickness. Cut the straps along the hide's spine. Straps that are cut from the belly to the spine become uneven in quality, lose shape and get stretched. If you need straps in a sturdy leather that does not stretch, you should use the hide's croupon, the back along the spine of the hide. Before using the strap cutter, you must make a clean cut along the spine so that you get a straight cut to put the strap cutter against. Use a rotary cutter, ruler and large cutting mat for this.

»——→ HOLE PUNCHING AND PIERCING

Almost every project will require you to make holes in the leather. They could be round holes for rivets or oblong holes to thread straps through. For hole punching, two tools are typically used: the revolving punch and the round punch.

I recommend that you start by investing in a revolving punch because it is more useful overall. Buy a good quality one; my experience is that the cheaper ones get dull quickly. If you need to make an oblong hole, you can make two round holes at a suitable distance from each other and then cut with a hobby knife (or a Stanley knife blade and rawhide mallet) between the two holes. It requires some practice to get it perfect, but it is an alternative to buying more expensive punches.

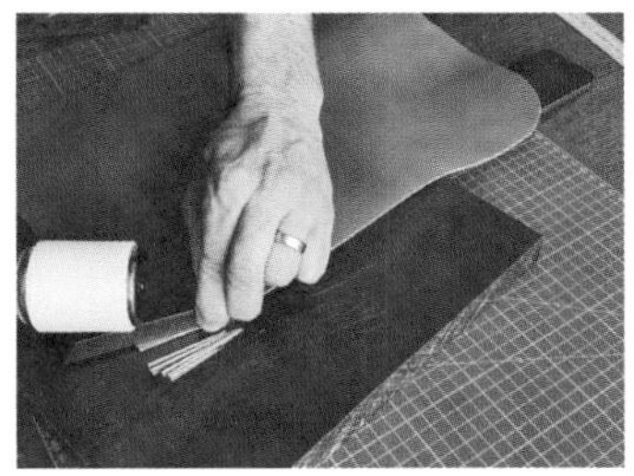

A Stanley knife blade can be used instead of a hobby knife to cut rounded corners.

TIPS!

To help cut straps from thinner, softer leather with a strap cutter, a 1–1.5 mm piece of leather can be inserted between the crossing strut where the straight blade sits and the strap cutter's handle (forming a V-shape). In this way, the crossing strut and the blade will be angled slightly and will "feed" the leather into the cutter. Note: The leather piece must be removed when cutting thicker leather.

»——→ TOOLS FOR HOLE PUNCHING AND PIERCING

REVOLVING PUNCH A revolving punch is a tong-grip tool with a rotating head. Around the revolving head, there are small round punches of varying sizes, usually 1–6 mm. The punch makes round holes, and the advantage is that you can choose from several hole sizes in one tool.

SINGLE PUNCH A single punch is used with a rawhide mallet and a cutting mat underneath as a base. A single punch can only make holes of the same size. Unlike the revolving punch, single punches come in different shapes: round, oblong, keyhole and teardrop. Making teardrop-shaped holes in a belt can give it a professional look. Punches made in the United States and Europe are expensive, but cheaper punches in different forms are available on the Internet and are often made in Asia.

END PUNCH An end punch is another punch tool used along with a rawhide mallet or hammer and slab for punching. End punches are available in various shapes and sizes and are used to cut off the ends of straps and belts. For straps, you can use an end punch with either a U-shaped cut or a more pointed one, but slightly rounded cuts call for an English point end punch. End punches are also available in a version for round corners, which makes it easier to cut round corners evenly and yields better results than a hobby knife. Just like other punches, good end punches are expensive. Cheaper ones made in China are sold online and are usually sold in sets with different sizes or different radiuses for cutting round corners.

SLAB OR CUTTING BOARD FOR PUNCHING Do not forget to use a slab or cutting board when working with punching tools to protect both your tools and workbench. With time and use, however, the slab or cutting board will develop protrusions from the punching tools you use, and, if you need to turn the hair side to the mat, these raised parts make marks on your leather. I recommend that you put an extra piece of leather between the slab and your project when using punching tools and pricking irons.

»——→ DYEING AND PAINTING

One of the benefits of vegetable-tanned leather is that it is easy to dye. For dyeing leather, there are acrylic-, water- and solvent-based paints, and these can be used as a coating, a leather dye or both. A coating paint or dye settles on top of the leather and forms a solid surface. Leather dye is a thinner dye that penetrates into the leather.

ACRYLIC PAINT A water-based, fast-drying paint. It is light-resistant, does not age and does not become brittle or crack. Acrylic paint is available in many different colors, and color nuances are often brilliant and clear. Acrylic paint is best suited for decorative painting and is applied with a brush. It does not penetrate down into the leather, but acts more as a topcoat. It can be thinned with water to get it to more easily penetrate the leather, but the effect is not the same as with leather dye.

SOLVENT-BASED PAINT A coating of solvent-based paint is best applied using a compressed air paint sprayer and spray nozzle. Solvent-based leather dye is most easily applied with a dauber. During my time at the shoemaker's, it was not uncommon for customers to want their shoes dyed. After cleaning the shoe with acetone, it was primed with leather dye and then coated with a solid color. In this way, a brown shoe could become black. The advantage of solvent-based dyes is that they stay better. They will withstand sunlight and wear better than water-based paints. The major drawback is that they are harmful to health and require expensive equipment to apply them. In addition to compressed air and a paint sprayer, a paint mask and adequate ventilation in the form of an extraction fan should be used.

WATER-BASED DYE For hobby use, I recommend penetrating water-based leather dye, so the advice about dyeing and painting in the following section refers only to this type of dye. As I said, the characteristics of leather dyes are unlike those of coating paints. It is thinner and slightly transparent if you apply it in small quantities. Here you can choose for yourself the color you want your leather to be by applying the dye in multiple coats. You can also dilute water-based leather dye with ammonia or denatured alcohol to enable it to penetrate deeper into the leather. This is necessary if your leather is conditioned or treated with oils at the tannery. Because vegetable-tanned leather darkens even when it is dyed, dyed leather will not have the same color after being exposed to sunlight and use. Sunlight can darken the leather, but it also causes the leather dye to fade.

TIPS!

Natural-colored vegetable leather is vulnerable to dirt, grease and scratches from fingernails. If you want to be extra careful with your leather, you can wear a pair of white cotton gloves while working. Then the leather remains spotless and your project will look completely unused when it is finished.

THINGS TO CONSIDER BEFORE YOU DYE

It is expensive to buy full sides of leather. Whether it is best to purchase a side of dyed leather from a tannery or to dye it yourself depends on how much leather you need. A full side of leather, dyed or undyed, can cost between $85 and $300, depending on the thickness and quality. A small container of leather dye, however, costs only $10 to $30, so it's more economical to buy undyed leather, (natural-colored), then dye the amount you need for yourself.

But if you want to have a full side of black leather, I recommend that you buy it from the tannery. The advantage of buying dyed leather directly from the tannery is that it is dyed a deeper tone, because the leather dye has penetrated further into the leather. This is visible when you cut a piece of leather dyed in the tannery and compare it with a piece of leather you dyed yourself, but be aware that the leather you buy from the tannery will also be subsequently treated with oils or waxes and that oil-treated leather is difficult to glue.

Leather can, if necessary, be treated at the tannery to hide defects. When you dye leather, it may be useful to know that the end result will be more even in a leather whose hair side is untreated. A leather that has been treated or sanded to hide defects often gets uneven tones when dyed. The dye is absorbed and becomes darker where the leather is sanded or treated. Before you start dyeing large pieces of leather, you should test your leather dye on smaller pieces of material to see how it is absorbed into the leather, if it can withstand water and so on. Set a small piece of dyed leather on the window sill for a sunny week during the summer to see how sunlight makes the leather darken and lightens the dye.

HOW TO DYE

Protect your clothes and the table when you dye leather. It may be possible to remove water-based dyes, but you have to be quick before they have time to dry. Once they have dried, they are difficult or impossible to wash off. Protect the surfaces around your work space, and make sure your space is flat and large enough. Larger pieces of leather can be moved, but it is easiest if the leather fits in your work space. Your work surface should be protected with plastic and paper. Avoid newspaper because the ink will bleed onto the leather. The floor and walls should also be covered, if you wish to protect them. Even if you think you can manage to avoid spilling or splashing, it is so easy to have a mishap. Open a window for ventilation and ensure that you have access to water to wipe off any spills and splashes.

The leather to be dyed must be free of grease and dirt. Natural, undyed leather easily absorbs grease and oil, which keeps the dye from penetrating into the leather. It is possible to remove grease stains by gently rubbing diluted oxalic acid (5 ml oxalic acid diluted with 0.5 L of water) onto the leather with a clean folded cotton cloth. Protective gloves are necessary, and you should keep oxalic acid in a cabinet that is out of reach of children because it is toxic. The easiest way to avoid needing to use oxalic acid is by taking care of your leather. Store it in a dry place, protected from dust, grease and sunlight. Do not mix undyed leather with colored leather, as the dyed leather may stain the undyed leather. If you store leather that has been treated with oil at the tannery with natural-colored leather, you are guaranteed to get grease stains on the untreated material.

When you have fixed up a good work space and your leather is clean from dirt and grease, it is time to begin to dye your leather. Do not forget to open the window for ventilation. Lay the leather on a flat surface so you can easily reach the entire surface. Fold a clean cotton cloth and dip it carefully in the leather dye. Remove excess dye by pressing the cloth gently against a piece of scrap leather. Start at a corner and apply the dye in small circular motions, being careful to spread the dye evenly. Remove excess dye and fill with more dye as needed. When you have dyed the entire surface, turn your leather 90 degrees and start again.

Multiple coats are often better than a full heavy coat, and it can be useful to dilute the dye with water.

Remember to first dye as much of the leather as you will need and then cut the leather for your patterns. That way you do not risk getting dye on the leather's back side or edges, which makes it difficult to glue.

GLUING

In several of the projects in this book you will glue together two or more pieces of leather and then sew them with saddle stitching. For leather, both solvent- and water-based contact adhesive are used, but I always recommend the latter. Solvent-based adhesives can be better if the joint is not to be sewn or if the leather is subjected to moisture during use, as in shoe soles. Many times during my time as a shoemaker, I stood over a glue container for hours, which resulted in light dizziness. With that being said, solvent-based contact adhesives can be purchased at most paint and hardware stores; however, be aware that it is hazardous, volatile and requires good ventilation. It can also be purchased in larger containers and can be poured into smaller plastic bottles where the spout of the bottle can be adjusted to the desired amount. If you choose to use solvent-based adhesives, be sure to read the warnings on the container and always seal the tube when not in use!

WATER-BASED CONTACT ADHESIVE

Water-based contact adhesives intended for leather are available in tubes or in small plastic jars with screw caps in hobby stores or on the Internet. They are environmentally friendly, less toxic and easy to use.

To apply the adhesive, I use the cheapest brushes from the paint store. The broadness of the brush you need is determined by what is to be glued, but a few brushes with a width of 1–3 cm can be good to have on hand. The bristle length of ordinary paint brushes are usually too long for gluing, so to make the brush less soft and pliable, I usually cut it down to just over 1 cm, preferably with a slight angle to make the bonding in corners and angles easier. Stiffer bristles make it easier to work with the adhesive. The brushes you use with a water-based adhesive can be rinsed with water and reused as long as the adhesive has not dried.

Besides brushes there are also plastic applicator sticks, available in various widths with a slightly angled tip to facilitate application at the corners. The advantage of glue applicators is that you can glue straighter and more accurately. You can also "push" the adhesive down into the leather to get a smooth glued surface. It is also possible to completely rinse off all adhesive residue from the applicators with lukewarm water.

Always close the container of the adhesive when not using it, otherwise the water will evaporate and the glue will become thick and difficult to work with.

HOW TO APPLY THE ADHESIVE

Before applying the adhesive, the surfaces must be clean and free of dirt, dust and grease. When you buy leather for your project, it is important to know that leather which has been re-fatted or oiled during the tanning process can't be glued. Contact adhesive does not sink into the leather but rather settles on top of the fat in the leather, making it impossible to properly adhere. Please check with the tannery or your supplier to see if the leather is pre-treated with oil or wax. Leather that has been re-fatted at the tannery has a softer feel than leather that is not treated with oil and wax, and this softer leather is excellent for belts and straps, for example, that can be assembled without glue. To avoid the risk of ruining the surfaces to be bonded, I recommend that you wait before oiling your own projects. If you want to rub oil into your leather, do it as a final touch – the icing on the cake.

Once you have checked that you have clean, smooth surfaces, mark the exact location on the leather where you will apply the adhesive. To mark the location, I usually draw carefully with the tip of an awl. Once your glue surfaces are marked, rough them up with coarse sandpaper – a grain size of 100–180 works well. A coarse emery board also works well because it is firmer than normal sandpaper and it is easier to sand following your markings with a sturdy file instead of the softer sand paper. Be sure to roughen the hair side that is to be glued, which has a shinier surface that must be sanded away for the adhesive to penetrate the leather.

Once your glue surfaces are marked and roughed up with sandpaper or a file, it's time to brush off any remnants of the sanded leather and apply the adhesive. Lay the leather pieces to be glued onto colorless, preferably waxed, paper. Avoid newspaper or colored paper as these can discolor the leather. If you use adhesive from a tube and the opening is small, you can squeeze a small amount onto a piece of paper, which you can then dip the brush in. Small surfaces obviously require less adhesive. When you glue bigger pieces, you can squeeze the glue directly onto the surfaces you marked. Then use the clipped brush or applicator stick to spread the adhesive evenly over the surfaces. The glue should be applied evenly and thinly and must be spread with a certain firmness so that it does not just end up on top of the leather – adhesion will be best if the glue has sunk into the leather. Remember not to spread the glue beyond the surfaces you marked.

Glue that is applied too thickly cannot be treated afterwards, and as contact adhesive dries quickly, trying to fix it afterwards is not recommended. The gluing process requires some practice. First, test how to best apply the adhesive with a brush or an applicator stick so that you get the right amount. It can be tempting to speed up a project, but your accuracy will determine the result. Better to have failed at gluing on some scrap pieces of leather than on a project that you put time and money into.

JOINING

After you have applied the adhesive and let it dry, it's time to put the two leather pieces together. Preferably, check the adhesive by carefully feeling the glued surfaces: They should feel slightly sticky (water-based adhesive) or completely dry (solvent-based adhesive). Avoid touching them too much because your body oils, dust, and dirt can impair the adhesion process. When the adhesive feels right, put together the glued surfaces. If possible, use your marks or the leather's outer edges to get the pieces to fit together exactly. Once you put together two glued surfaces, they cannot be readjusted. If you have done good preparation work, it will glue very well. If you have to subsequently pull apart two glued surfaces that are not put together as you wanted, you have to start over by sanding and cleaning off the adhesive residue. Leather pieces can be stretched out of shape when you pull them apart after being glued. It is important to get the joining exact on the first attempt.

When the leather pieces are glued and put together in the way you want them, they must then be pressed. Avoid using tools such as hammers, because they leave permanent dents in the leather. Instead, I usually use a roller tool or a glass slicker, a centimeter-thick piece of glass with polished edges that are rounded and smooth (it's also known in Sweden by the unflattering name, "rubbing whore"). To protect the project you're working on from marks when you use the roller, place a piece of leather between the roller and the project. If you use a glass slicker, you can rub or press directly onto the glued leather. It is important that you use firm, even pressure over the entire joined area. An alternative to the roller and glass slicker is to press the glued pieces together with paper clips, which works best when gluing along the edges. You can find simple inexpensive clips at an office supply store. Because paper clips can make marks on the leather, they must be covered with pieces of leather. Glued pieces must be pressed together, so let the clips remain in place until it is time for the next step: saddle stitching. If you accidentally get adhesive in unwanted places, the adhesive can be rubbed off with a piece of rubber eraser.

RIVETS AND SNAPS

To join leather, a rivet or snap can also be a solution. Rivets and snaps come in different forms, ranging from the simple old-fashioned copper rivet to push snaps with fine embellishments. Some rivets and snaps require special tools to set, but others are easier to attach and require only a screwdriver or a hammer and a hard surface. For hobby work, I recommend hand tools, but there are also more expensive machines that make fastening rivets easier with less risk of failure.

CHICAGO SCREW A rivet that is practical and easy to set since the two parts are screwed together. If you use a pair of pliers to hold the top, you need to protect the screw so that it does not get damaged by the pliers. To prevent it from coming loose, a drop of Loctite in the threads helps.

CONCHOS Large decorative buttons that come in an assortment of variations, including stars, skulls and coins. Most are available with a screw attachment and can easily replace the top on a dull Chicago screw.

DECORATIVE STUD Just like it sounds, a decorative stud is for decorating leather. There are a multitude of different varieties, and most are attached to the leather by two or more tabs on the stud's back that go through the leather, and then are bent so that the rivet is fixed in place.

DOUBLE RIVET Used to join two pieces of leather, but it can also be used as a decorative detail. The advantage of using a double rivet is that it is fastened better than a decorative stud. The disadvantage is that it is not made in as many decorative shapes. The double rivet has a top and bottom. Both parts have a cap. As with snaps, it requires a special tool to fasten double rivets so that they retain their shape.

BUTTON STUD Used in the same way as the snap: to close or fasten two pieces of leather. It is attached to the leather that sits underneath and is threaded through a keyhole-shaped hole in the upper leather piece so it can act as a lock or buckle for a bag or a bracelet. Button studs are available with screw fasteners or rivet fasteners. Both are easy to attach, and you only need a screwdriver or rawhide mallet and a hard surface such as a slab for punching.

COPPER RIVET The traditional copper rivet has a nail-like base and a top piece consisting of a disc. The neck of the rivet is passed through the leather from the bottom and the disc is then slipped over the neck. The neck of the rivet is then flattened with a striker or setter and rawhide mallet. To get a good result, the length of the rivet neck should be neither too short nor too long. It should stick up a few millimeters past the disc before it is flattened.

MAGNETIC SNAP Can be used to invisibly close or lock. Just as with the decorative stud, it is set with two or more prongs passing through the leather and then further through a disc at the back of the leather. The prongs are then bent to set the snap in place. The second half of the snap is set in a similar fashion.

SNAP FASTENER The snap has a top and bottom consisting of two parts each. Setting the snap requires a special tool that can be adapted to the size of the snap. The tool for the

snap's top part or cap has a concave dome in the metal that is customized to the round cap. The snap's cap is placed in the domed anvil tool and retains its shape when you hit the top of it with a hammer. Similarly, there is a tool with a tip adapted to the bottom of the snap. Keep each tool with the corresponding parts of each snap so you do not mix them up and mismatch tools and parts. Sometimes a snap setting will be unsuccessful and you will need to remove it and set a new one. A wire cutter may work, but avoid catching the leather with the blades because leather is easily damaged. A small power tool with a grinding wheel that works on metal does the best job. Grind down the part that holds the snap together. Be careful not to let the snap get too hot and burn the leather.

EYELET The eyelet is used to reinforce the leather around a hole or to decorate for a more stylized impression. Eyelets are made in a variety of sizes and consist of two metal rings, a top and bottom piece. The top has a neck or post that is threaded through the leather, and the bottom is a ring that is placed around the post on the back of the leather. For securing eyelets, a special tool is required for each eyelet size. Hitting the eyelet with a rawhide mallet on the eyelet-setter or spreader flattens the post outward and clamps to the ring on the back of the leather

SADDLE STITCHING

Compared to machine stitching, saddle stitching is more time consuming to perform, but it lasts much longer. There are many different types of machine stitches, but perhaps the most common consists of an upper and lower thread that interlock in the material being sewn. The threads on the top and bottom never go completely through the material. The weakness in a machine stitch is that the entire seam gets pulled out if one thread breaks – we have all pulled on a thread on the top or underside of a machine-sewn garment and observed how the entire seam comes loose. Saddle stitching consists of two stitches, but its greater strength is that the same thread passes back and forth through the leather and thus forms both the upper and lower thread. If a thread breaks, the leather is held in place by the other thread. Mending saddle stitching is also easier because the desired seam length can be replaced with new thread and an "invisible" knot. Broken machine stitching, on the other hand, often unravels entirely and must be resewn. Saddle stitching is also better suited than the machine for repairing machine stitching. A machine-stitched wallet, for example, is sewn in several steps. If the wallet needs to be repaired, it can be difficult or impossible to fit it into the machine. At that point, hand-sewn saddle stitching is the only choice.

STITCH POSITIONING

The spacing between seam stitches and how far from the edge you choose to place your seam is a question of durability, aesthetics and design. When you're deciding on the spacing between stitches, consider whether your project will be subjected to stress. Stitches that are too close together make the leather weaker because you perforate or partially cut off the leather as you sew. That is why a belt should not be sewn crosswise over the leather. To maintain the leather's strength, stitches should not sit closer than 2 mm or 13 stitches per inch (2.54 cm). Items that are not going to carry a load or be subjected to stress can, of course, be sewn with closer stitching than that. Another factor that controls the stitch spacing is thread thickness. A thicker thread generally requires more spacing between stitches than a thinner thread.

As for where the seam should be relative to the edge of the leather, a simple guideline is to place the seam the same distance from the edge as the thickness of the glued leather. If the joined leather pieces to be sewn are 3 mm

SADDLE STITCHING

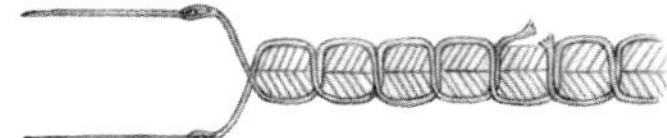

In saddle stitching, the same thread passes all the way through the leather and thus forms a seam that does not unravel if the thread breaks.

Machine stitching has two threads that never pass all the way through the leather, so the entire seam can unravel.

thick, make the seam 3 mm from the edge. However, this is only a rule of thumb: For stitching leather that is 7 mm thick, for example, you don't have to make the seam 7 mm from the edge; in such cases you can let aesthetics decide.

⋙⟶ TOOLS AND MATERIALS

STITCHING GROOVER A stitching groover has a sharp cupped cut that makes a rounded groove in the leather. The groove makes it easier to make the stiches straight and also protects the seam that is recessed in the groove. To make it easier to keep the groove at a uniform distance from the edge of the leather, the stitch groover has an adjustable guide. An alternative to a stitch groover is to use a scratch compass or gauge compass to mark an even line along the edge of the leather where you want to stitch. If you use a compass with a sharp tip, the seam ends up on top of the leather and gets worn more easily.

PRICKING IRON A pricking iron is used to make holes for your seam stitches and has sharp, angled, diamond-shaped teeth or points. Pricking irons are available with a different number of teeth and with various distances between the teeth. You place it into the groove you made with the stitch groover or the line from the compass and then hit it through the leather with a rawhide mallet, then move the pricking iron forward so that the last tooth of the iron stands in the first hole you just made. That way you get an even spacing between the holes. Work toward yourself with the pricking iron so that you have a good view and can place the holes exactly on your mark. Be sure to keep the pricking iron at a 90-degree angle to the leather so that the holes come out on the leather's under side in a straight line. For heavier leather, you will need to finish the hole with a diamond awl. To protect the slab from being full of small raised holes, you can add a thicker piece of leather between the slab and your project when you use the pricking iron. If you do not use a piece of leather as an extra base, the raised holes on the slab caused by the pricking iron can make ugly marks in the leather you are working on.

STITCHING WHEEL A stitching wheel is used to mark where you will make the seam stitches with a diamond awl, if you do not use a pricking iron. First, dampen the leather to be marked with a damp sponge. Then allow the stitching wheel to run in the groove you made with the stitching groover or on the line from the compass to mark where you will make the stitches with the sewing awl. Like the pricking irons, there are stitching wheels with different spacing between the stitch marks.

DIAMOND AWL This is an awl with a diamond-shaped tip that is used to make stitch holes in the seam. Skilled and experienced saddle makers use only one sewing awl to make regular, even stitches, but a pricking iron can be helpful if you do leatherworking as a hobby. An awl is used on thicker leather to complete the hole started by the pricking iron so it goes all the way through the leather. It is important that the sewing awl is sharpened to more easily penetrate through the thick leather. A simple whetstone for kitchen knives works great when you need to sharpen your sewing awl. The handle of the sewing awl is either completely round or round with a faceted, flat side. The benefit of a handle with a flat side is that, when the sewing blade is screwed in, the flat side of the blade lines up with the flat side of the handle. This makes it easier to make your seam stitch at the correct angle.

LINEN THREAD Linen thread is a natural material, which makes it more attractive than synthetic thread. The disadvantage is that it doesn't last as long – it dries and deteriorates after anywhere from five to twenty years. For those who do not want to wax the linen thread, thread that has already been waxed can be purchased.

SYNTHETIC THREAD Synthetic thread is more rigid than linen thread. It does not stretch and lasts the longest, but aesthetically it may be less appealing simply because it is synthetic. When you have finished sewing, you can knot or seal the synthetic thread easily by heating the end with a lighter so that a ball of melted thread is formed. Be careful when melting the end so that the heat from the lighter does not melt the finished seam. Like linen thread, synthetic thread can be bought already waxed.

BEESWAX Beeswax is used primarily to increase linen thread's durability, but it also prevents fraying during sewing. A linen thread that is not treated with beeswax deteriorates quickly if it comes in contact with moisture. When you prepare the needles and thread, treat the linen thread by rubbing a piece of wax over it when it is taut.

SADDLE STITCHING STEP BY STEP

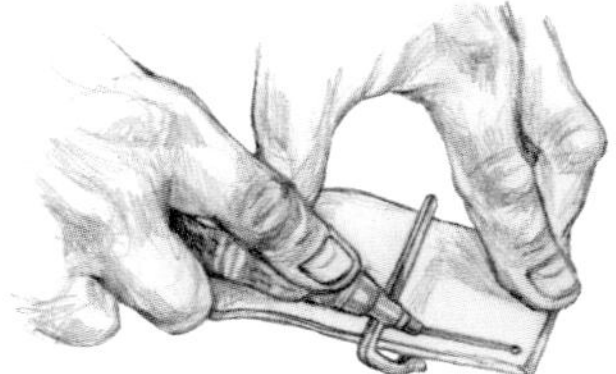

STEP 1

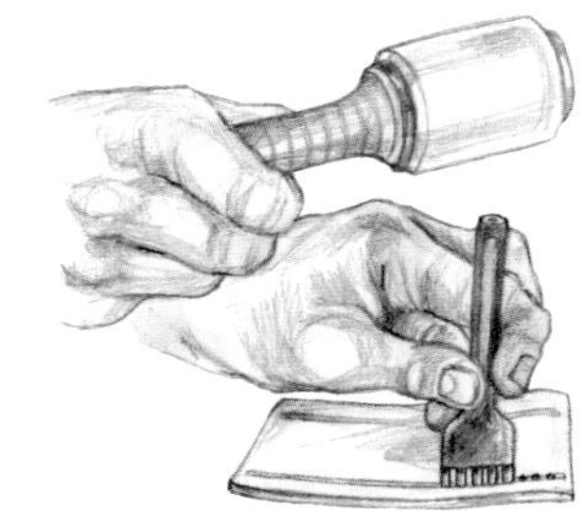

STEP 2

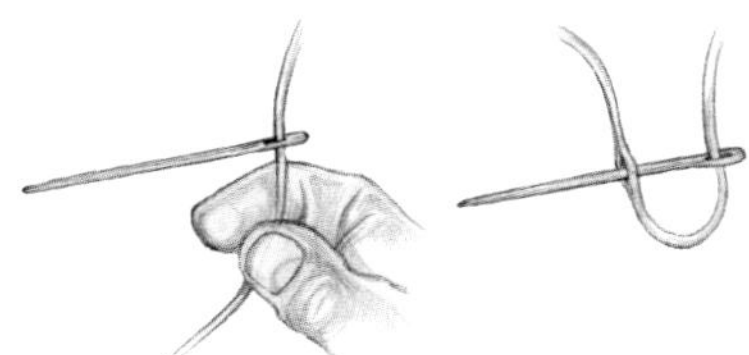

STEP 4.1

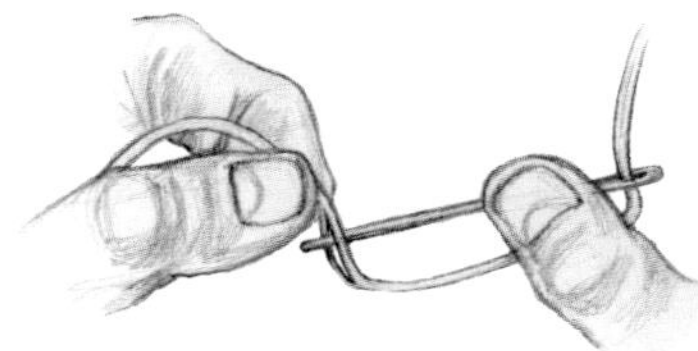

STEP 4.2

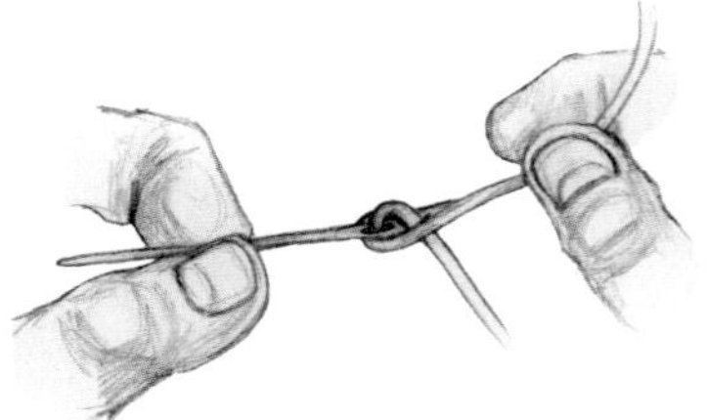

STEP 4.3

HARNESS NEEDLES As mentioned earlier, harness needles used for saddle stitching have blunt tips. The blunt tip is so that the needle doesn't damage the thread when it passes through the finished hole or stitch. If a needle penetrates the other thread, pull out the threads and make sure the pierced thread is still intact. If the pierced thread is damaged, you should back up and pull out enough stitches to knot or seal it where the thread is undamaged, and then start all over again with the new thread. There is no universal measurement for needles and thread. The size of the needles have different numbers in different countries. The needle, thread, and stitch spacing you choose is a question of durability, aesthetics and design. Take a look at various leather items to get an idea of what you like best.

STITCHING PONY, LEATHERCRAFT CLAMP, OR SADDLER'S STITCHING HORSE A stitching pony is used to hold small pieces to be sewn in place so that you have both hands free while stitching. Stitching ponies or leathercraft clamps are available in different sizes depending on how large the leather pieces are. A saddler's stitching horse is a sewing stool and is suitable for larger jobs. To protect the leather when it is held in the clamp, you can secure a piece of leather in the clamp's "mouth." Bulky or larger, heavier projects that cannot be clamped in a stitching horse can be placed on your lap or on a table instead.

»——› HOW TO DO SADDLE STITCHING

STEP 1 Mark the leather where you want to sew by making a groove with a stitching groover or a line with a compass.

STEP 2 Use a pricking iron to make your holes: Put the iron into the groove from the stitching groover or on the line from the compass and carefully tap the pricking iron through the leather with a rawhide mallet. Stronger leather may need a follow-up with a diamond awl.

STEP 3 Start by measuring out the thread for your seam. The basic rule is that the length of the thread should be about three times the length of the seam you are going to sew. If the seam is only a few centimeters, the thread must of course be three times longer than that. You must have enough thread to secure the thread in the needle with a few extra needle lengths of thread remaining. The length of the thread is also determined by the thickness of the leather to be sewn; thicker leather requires longer thread.

STEP 4 For saddle stitching, use two needles of equal size attached to each end of the same thread. To secure the thread in the needle to prevent it from coming loose while sewing, pass the thread through the needle's eye, then pierce through the other end of the thread and pull it down over the needle. Do the same with the second needle. Sometimes the waxed thread may be difficult to thread through the needle's eye. One tip is to gently pull the end of the thread with a needle or awl to flatten it. If the end of the thread unravels, you can rub it over a piece of beeswax and flatten it again.

STEP 5 Decide where you are going to start and finish your seam. To sew all the way around a piece of leather, you will finish where you started. Since you finish the seam with double stitches, you will want to begin and end where it is least visible, if possible. Later in this book I give tips on how you can start and finish your seam at an edge.

STEP 6 Fasten the leather you are going to sew in the stitching pony with the leather's front side against your right hand and the back side against your left hand. The side that was facing up when you made holes with the pricking iron was the front side of the leather. Make sure the stitch hole you are going to start your seam with is located a few centimeters above the stitching pony's far corner.

STEP 7 Start by threading one of the needles through the hole (hole 1) you want to begin your seam with. Make sure you have the same amount of thread on both sides of the stitch hole. If the thread is 100 cm, you must have 50 cm of thread on each side of the leather. From now on, we will refer to the needle that starts every stitch from the back side of the leather as needle A, and the needle completing each stitch on the front side of the leather as needle B.

STEP 8 Always sew the saddle stitch toward yourself. Draw needle A halfway through the next hole (hole 2) closest to you.

STEP 9 Put needle B behind needle A. Now take needle A so that you are holding both needle A and needle B together between your thumb and index finger.

STEP 10 With both needles in your grip, pull needle A all the way through the hole (hole 2), but don't pull the entire thread through the hole yet. Next, turn the hand with the needles remaining in your grip so that needle B points against the same hole (hole 2). Hold the thread away from needle A with your other hand so that it does not get pierced by needle B. Then place needle B in the same hole. Be sure to place the needle so that it is between you and the thread from needle A. (The holes from the pricking iron are at an angle so that the seam will form the characteristic saddle stitch pattern.) The thread that comes from the back side should then be threaded through the leather in the hole's upper side. The thread coming from the front side should be threaded through the leather in the hole's lower part, which is closest to you.

STEP 11 Insert needle B in hole 2. Hold the thread away from needle A with your other hand so that it is not pierced by needle B.

STEP 12 Grasp needle B with your left hand and pull it through hole 2.

STEP 13 Now pull the threads from both needle A and needle B through hole 2. When you have pulled both threads through, draw them tight by pulling the thread upward on the front side

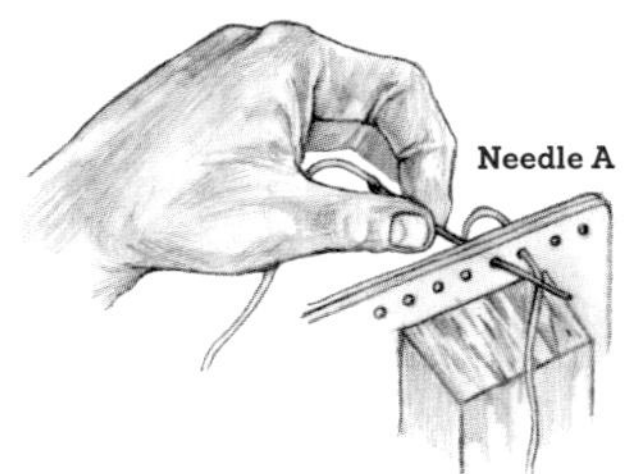

STEP 8

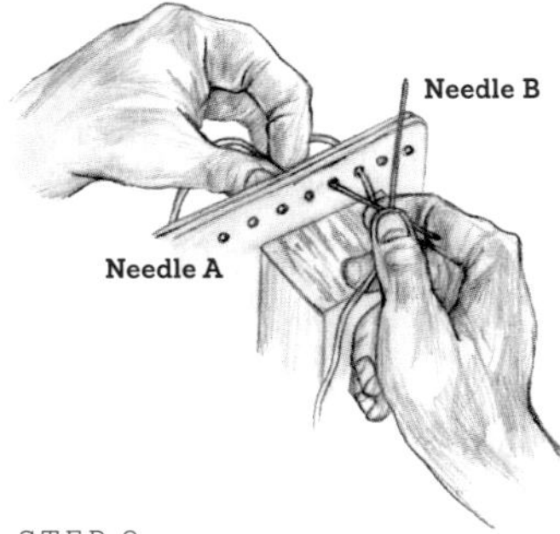

STEP 9

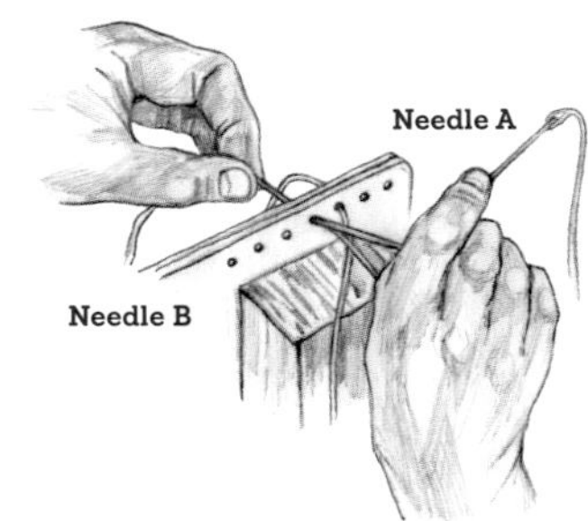

STEP 10

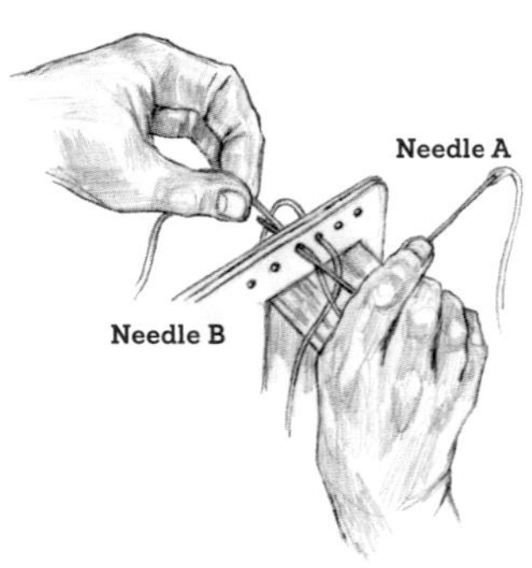

STEP 11

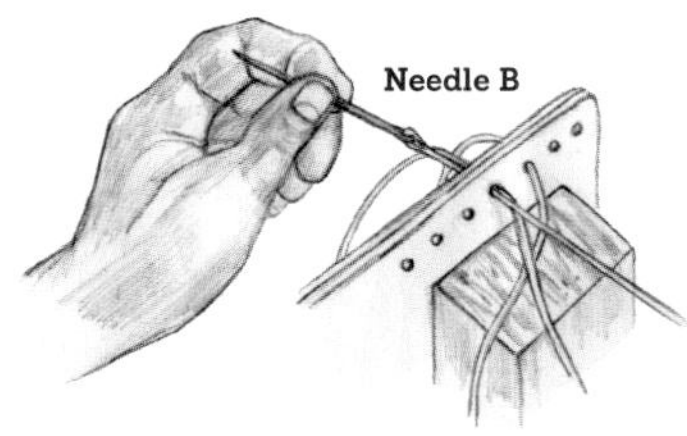

STEP 12

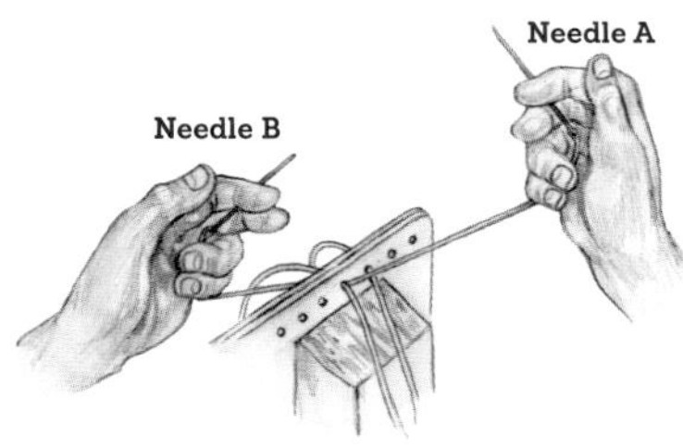

STEP 13

of the leather and by pulling the thread downward on the back side of the leather. Keep in mind that softer and thinner leather puckers up along the seam if you pull too tight.

STEP 14 Repeat steps 8 to 13 for holes 3, 4, 5, 6 and so on until you are ready to secure the thread.

STEP 15 Secure the thread by sewing double stitches with both needles A and B in hole 1 and with needle B in hole 2. Make sure both threads come out on the leather's back side. Cut the threads a few millimeters from the back side of the leather. If you are using synthetic thread, you can heat the ends with a lighter so that they melt and then press them together before they have dried.

TO START AND FINISH A SEAM AT AN EDGE

A seam that's made along an edge does not always end where it starts. For instance, to make a credit card case, you have to sew around three edges and leave the top edge open. With such a seam, I think it looks best if the seam is symmetrical, meaning that it both starts and ends with double stitches. Here, there are two options. The first option is to start the stitch by threading needle A through hole 2, and then sewing two stitches away from yourself out to the edge of the case. Put the threads from needles A and B around the edge and continue with holes 1, 2, 3, 4 and so on according to steps 8 to 13. The second option is to not let the threads go around the edge. Start in hole 3, sew two stitches away from you and then turn around and sew toward you around the entire case. Now the first two stitches are at the beginning of the double seam. When you fasten the thread at the other edge of the case, do it exactly the same way as when you started. Reverse two stitches and fasten the threads according to step 15.

»——› EDGE FINISHING

To obtain a decorative finish around the edges of a project, there are two tools for edging: the wooden creaser and the metal creasing iron. A wooden creaser is a handle made of wood with two angled edges on each end. The four edges are of different widths. Mark the edges by putting one of the edges of the creasing tool with the desired width against the leather edge and pulling the creaser along the edge.

Creasing irons are available in adjustable or fixed versions. The adjustable creaser (or screw creaser) is adjusted with a screw. The creasing iron is also available with a wheel to make parallel marks on the leather. Heating the creasing iron over a flame will make the marks clearer. Natural-colored vegetable-tanned leather does well with edge finishing. For clearer marking, dampen the leather with a sponge before you mark it, but be careful! Wet leather is easy to make marks on, even in places that you weren't intending to mark. As always, it is a good idea to practice on scrap leather first. There are also more expensive and advanced creasing tools, similar to soldering irons, that are interchangeable. A soldering iron has the right temperature and can also be used to burn off synthetic thread when you secure your saddle stitching seam.

»—→ EDGE TRIMMING

To get a clean edge, or to prepare an edge for buffing, you will need to do some trimming. Edgers, edge bevelers, and edge trimmers are available in different widths with either straight or contoured blades. The width you choose depends on how thick the leather is; thicker leather usually requires a wider edger. Whether you choose straight or contoured blades depends on the desired result. For a belt with edges that will be buffed, I use a contoured blade that shapes and adapts the edges, along with a rounded polishing tool of the same width as the belt is thick. For best results, the edge of the blade must be sharp. A dull edger pushes the leather forward and makes the edge uneven. If the leather is of lower quality and a bit flimsy, it is almost impossible to get a nice edge if the edger is not sharp. It is difficult to cut the edge of leather that is thinner than 1.5 mm, but, on the other hand, it can be buffed without edge cutting.

Before you place the tool on the edge of the leather, it is important that the surface is clean and free of leather scraps. If there is something under the leather, the edger will catch on them and make ugly marks. It's also helpful if the leather to be cut is placed against an anvil or an edge. I always use a large cutting mat as a base underneath, and on top of that, I place a smaller cutting mat. By laying the side of the leather that will not be cut against the small cutting mat, I get a stop and a support all along the edge, making it easier to bring the edger forward with a steady, firm motion. Slide the edger along the edge with a constant pressure at a 45-degree angle. The longer you can cut without lifting up and starting again, the smoother the edge will be. You can stop and start again but long, even cuts tend to be the best. It is a good idea to practice on a piece of scrap leather before starting in earnest.

TIPS!

To get a nice finish on your project's burnished edges, rub a piece of beeswax over the edges and then rub them lightly with a cotton cloth.

EDGE BURNISHING

Burnishing, or edge buffing, is done to close the pores of the leather edges or surfaces. The heat generated by the friction closes the pores of the leather and gives a nice glossy, smooth surface. You may prefer to leave the raw, untreated surface – it is a matter of taste. But if you want to achieve a more elegant result, the solution is to burnish the edges.

It is worth considering that a dyed, vegetable-tanned leather is not always fully colored all the way through, and it may be necessary to dye the edge first and then burnish it. If you use a natural-colored vegetable-tanned leather, the edge does not need to be dyed. Natural-colored leather will get a darker tone after burnishing, which describes very well what actually happens: The leather gets a slightly "burned" edge.

To burnish an edge, use a piece of rough white canvas or a burnishing tool. For an authentic look, it should be burnished entirely by hand, but there is an easier alternative in the form of small cocobolo wood burnishing tips that are fitted for the Dremel power tool. Burnishing tips are available in various widths depending on the leather thickness; suggestions on where to buy these can be found on page 125.

Leather workshops use a type of drill that is fixed in place and tips that are larger in diameter than hand tools. The advantage of larger tips is that they do not dig into the leather as easily. Another advantage is that you have two hands free to hold your work. If you use a power tool, the burnishing tip must be applied with a steady and solid pace over the leather's edge, otherwise you risk burning the leather. The leather will become dark brown and the surface will crack easily.

BEFORE YOU BURNISH

Before you begin to burnish, the leather must be prepped. A rough cut strap for a belt has perpendicular edges. In order for your polishing tools to be able to shape or round off the edge, it must be shaved down with an edging tool. Instructions for using an edger can be found on page 38. For optimal results, you should also sand the edge with a fine sandpaper after you have trimmed it. Glued leather pieces have to be sanded with a coarse sandpaper, but follow with a nail file for edge trimming and fine sanding so that the edge is smooth and even before burnishing. A smoother, more even edge makes a big difference. Burnishing will also be easier.

After you trim the edge, you need to decide whether you want to dye it; a burnished edge cannot be dyed afterwards. For black- or brown-dyed leather, the dying of a cut edge must be done before it is burnished. Even with natural-colored leather, you can dye the edge if desired, but be careful not to get dye where you do not want it. Refillable sponges and pens can make it easier. Personally, I use a stipple brush or a paint dauber. In time, you will learn how much color and how fast you should draw your sponge or stipple brush over the edge to get a good result.

HOW TO BURNISH

After you have dyed the edge and the color has dried, it is time to prepare the edge for burnishing. By applying any form of liquid or fat, you make it easier for your burnishing tool to round the edges and to make sure that the edges do not get too hot and burn when you burnish them. There are different ways to prepare the leather. Gently rubbing in water and saddle soap, or water and glycerin, works well. There is also a special burnishing gum made of tragacanth that can be ordered on the Internet. Tragacanth is a natural product derived from the resin of certain legumes from the Middle East. In English, it is called tragacanth burnishing gum, and it comes in different colors. Transparent works well on leather that has been dyed. As with dyeing, it is important not to get the gum in places other than the edge you want to burnish. Gum that comes in contact with the leather's hair side clogs the pores of the leather and forms a film, which makes the leather hard to finish and treat.

Now it is time to start burnishing. If you use a hand tool or a canvas cloth, burnishing is strenuous and sweaty work, and having a firm grip on what you are burnishing is a must. You can hold larger jobs between your knees. If you select a burnishing tool, it should be of the same width as the edge you are burnishing. A tool that's too wide or too narrow doesn't fit against the entire edge and the result is uneven. Apply the polishing liquid to about 15 cm of the leather's edge and rub the tool quickly along the edge with a smooth firm pressure. You will soon notice that the edge's surface becomes smooth and glossy. If you use a Dremel-type power tool, the rate should be no more than 1500 rpm. A power tool makes burnishing much easier, and if the tool is also fixed in one position, you will have both hands free to move your leather back and forth across the polishing wheel. Remember that the power tool makes the liquid you used to pretreat the edge splatter off. If you used black tragacanth, chances are that you will have dark spots on the floor and walls. It is a good idea to cover the floor and walls with plastic before burnishing with power tools.

When finishing, you can rub beeswax over the burnished edge and then give it a final polishing with a cotton cloth.

SKIVING

Shaving down or reducing the thickness of edges or an end of the leather is called skiving and is done with a special skiving knife. Shaving the ends of the leather is necessary when joining together two pieces or trimming a strap or a belt before riveting or sewing it around the buckle. Skiving is also done when you want to fold and glue the edges of the leather that will be visible. It is important that the knife you use is sharp and that the blade is held at a 30-degree angle to the cutting direction. The surface must be hard, preferably a stone slab, so that the knife does not cut into it. The knife is placed where the shaving is to begin and is drawn out against the leather's edge. Invisible joints and smooth shaving on a leather project are the difference between the work of the amateur and the work of a master.

MOLDING

Vegetable-tanned leather is excellent for soaking and then molding to virtually any shape. The leather will retain that shape as long as it is not soaked again. During my years at the shoemaker's, I made many pairs of clogs. I began by nailing a mold onto a wooden sole, then I nailed the punched out vegetable-tanned leather that had been soaked in warm water around the mold. The extra leather was cut off, and after the leather had dried, the mold was removed, and a natural-colored wooden clog was finished.

There are two ways to do shaping; which way you do it depends not only on what you're making but also on how you want the finished product to look. For some projects, the form or mold can be inserted after the project has been sewn together. Other projects require you to shape your various pieces before sewing or joining them together.

To use a cell phone case as an example, you can glue and sew it together first, then get it wet and insert a mold that is made to the phone's exact measurements. The wet leather yields to the mold when you push it in. When the leather is dry, the mold is removed, and you can simply insert a cell phone. If you do not mold the case beforehand, you will have a hard time getting the cell phone inside.

You can also use the other molding method with the same cell phone case. Instead of inserting a mold of a cell phone into your finished case, you can shape the parts before gluing and sewing together the case. You can also make a leather sheath for a pocket knife by molding the front side of the sheath around the pocket knife, letting it dry, and then joining it to a flat back piece.

You can use different materials when making your molds. Just keep in mind that the mold must be able to withstand moisture. Softer wood, such as pine, swells up more with moisture than hardwood. For some of the thinner molds, as with those for cell phone cases, I have used plastic cutting boards that I sawed and sanded to the right size and shape. The advantage of plastic is that it does not swell or split. For thicker shapes, I have used wood or plywood that can withstand moisture.

»——› STAMPING

Vegetable-tanned leather is well-suited for stamping. Stamping is placing a pattern or ornamentation on the hair side of the leather using one or several stamping tools depending on the finished pattern design. Stamps are made of metal, and the patterned part is on the end of a rod that is approximately 10 centimeters long. Any contours are cut in the leather using a special knife with a movable blade. Then, a stamp pattern is struck into the soaked leather with a rawhide mallet.

I will not describe stamping in any more detail in this book, but for those who want to try it, the most common designs can be found in hobby shops. Since stamping is common in American saddle making, I recommend that those who want to develop their skills take a look at the different stamp designs sold by Barry King Tools in Sheridan, Wyoming.

If you want to put your own brand or company's name on the things you make, you can also order a stamp in the form of a seal on the Internet, if you have your logo in a PDF format. Then you can simply stamp the logo onto the damp leather just like any other stamp design.

»——› CREATE YOUR OWN

As your knowledge and skills in leather handcrafting increase, it is likely that your desire to make your own designs will increase. You will eventually get a feel for the leather and how you can shape it and create your own ideas. Perhaps you begin practicing on paper, or you can find inspiration from leather projects that you see in shops – it can be exciting to discover that you actually have enough knowledge to do much of what is sold in stores or on the Internet.

When designing your own projects, it is important to make well-planned choices, in terms of both form and function. Think through the entire project from start to finish. What kind of leather will you use? How thick will the leather be? How will it be attached? Where do you need to sew and where do you need fasteners or rivets? Will the straps on a bag be adjustable? Cutting the leather to your own designed projects and then discovering that you do not have the proportions you had in mind can be very frustrating. Try out your design on leather that you can spare. Test the form and function of a prototype before using your fine leather. Sometimes I have to make several prototypes and small adjustments before I am completely satisfied, especially if the project is advanced. Making mistakes can actually be useful experience for the next project.

Part three

BRAIDING

There are entire books that deal only with braiding leather and rawhide, including a 550-page reference book by Bruce Grant. What I describe in this book is just the tip of the iceberg. I go through a few simple flat braids and round braids as well as a few knots and buttons that you can use to finish your braid. All braiding is based on using the same kind of mathematical logic to form a symmetrical pattern. Once you've mastered the basics and the "thinking," you can easily develop your braiding project.

INTRODUCTION

The art of braiding and binding with leather straps, knots and decorative buttons has a thousand-year history that can be traced back to the Phoenicians. The Phoenician Empire was based in the eastern part of the Middle East, or present-day Lebanon, around 1600 BC. The Phoenicians were merchants and the best seafarers at that time. In competition with the Greeks, the Phoenician Empire expanded throughout northern Africa. The city of Carthage on the coast of present-day Tunisia became a thriving trade center, and the Phoenician Empire spread all the way to northwest Africa and the Moors. When the Moors occupied the Iberian Peninsula around 700 AD, the prominent Caliphate of Córdoba was created. Moorish culture valued beautiful, functional objects, and multiple trades in leatherworking emerged, including the art of making patterned and ornamented harnesses. The city of Córdoba today still lends its name to cordovan leather, a high-quality leather used in men's fine shoes. The Moors were expelled from the Iberian Peninsula during the 1300s and 1400s, but their knowledge of leatherworking survived. Then, when skilled Spanish leather workers came with Cortés and other colonists, they spread this knowledge to the Americas.

In Mexico, *vaqueros*, or cowboys, were experts at braiding, and for the horsemen, or *charros*, the horse was a central part of life, as was decorating it with detailed leather.

Braiding and the art of binding with leather are dying out. The form and function of yesterday has slowly been replaced with new solutions. The braided leather button and woven leather seam have been replaced by metal buttons or rivets. When humans find new solutions, the need for the old ways changes. Today, traditional knowledge lives on with a few "braiders," but knowledge and craft skills are likely to disappear when these artisans are gone.

All types of braids are made by repeating the same technique and following a pattern. Although it is not evident at first glance, there is a simple logic or mathematical pattern in every type of braid. Failure to follow the pattern creates an asymmetrical braid. The final result should look the same from all sides and be equilateral. You can of course change patterns during the braiding, provided that the change is consistent and made with all the strands in the braid.

The term "braiding" describes both the traditional flat braid and the round braid, the art of connecting leather with strands, making buttons and knots in leather and decorating leather. There are many different varieties of braids and braiding. In this book, we will only touch on traditional flat and round braids. I will leave the more intricate braiding techniques to the experts.

TOOLS FOR BRAIDING

The list of tools used for simple braiding are presented in this book. There are additional tools you may need if you continue with more advanced braids.

CUTTING BOARD AND CUTTING MAT
Surface for using knives and punches.

STRAP CUTTER Cuts belts to the desired width, and can cut down to about 1.5 mm in thickness. If you have the need for thinner leather, you can trim down the leather using a skiving machine, and then cut it into strands.

AWL Used to tighten or widen the distance between each of the strands to even the braid when it is finished. It can also be used to create an opening between the strands to help thread other strands through when braiding knots. An awl tool has a blunt tip and rounded edges to prevent damage to the leather when it is inserted between the strands.

STANLEY KNIFE BLADE The replaceable blade for a Stanley knife, used to make straight cuts on the cord for a magic braid, or to cut the end of a strap, instead of using a punch.

45°
60°

OBLONG PUNCH An elongated punch that can be used as an alternative to a knife to make holes in the strap for a hole braid.

RAWHIDE MALLET Used to strike punches without damaging them.

»——→ THREE SIMPLE BRAIDS

HOLE BRAID

The hole braid is not a braid in the traditional sense since it does not consist of multiple strands that are woven together – instead just one strand is used. Along the center line of the strand or strap, oblong holes are cut or punched and the two ends of the strap are alternately threaded through them.

TOOLS AND MATERIALS

oblong punch or hobby knife and revolving punch
slab for punching
strap cutter or ruler and rotary cutter
rawhide mallet
slide rule
cutting mat
Stanley knife blade

STEP 1 Start by cutting a belt to the desired width and length. Use a strap cutter for long straps, or a ruler and rotary cutter are fine for shorter straps.

STEP 2 To know where you will place your holes in step 3, measure or fold the belt in the middle. You will place the first hole from the strap's midpoint.

STEP 3 The size of the holes is determined by the strap's width and thickness. As an example, a strap that is 10 mm wide should have holes that are about 10–12 mm long. This works well on straps that are up to 2 mm in thickness. If a strap is thicker than 2 mm, it may require larger holes. The hole length also depends on how stiff or rigid the leather is; stiff and rigid leather may require larger holes. You can always try it out and judge for yourself what you think looks the best. To make the holes, use a utility knife or an oblong punch. If you use a utility knife, make holes at the end of each knife cut using the smallest hole of a revolving punch. A small hole in the end of each knife cut reduces the risk of the leather cracking. Make the first

HOLE BRAID

STEP 2

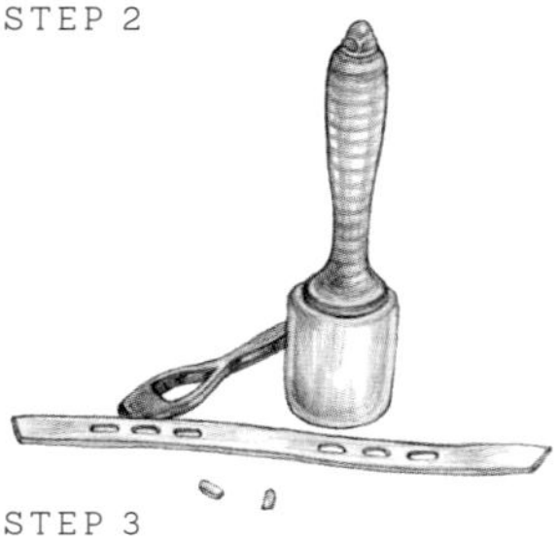

STEP 3

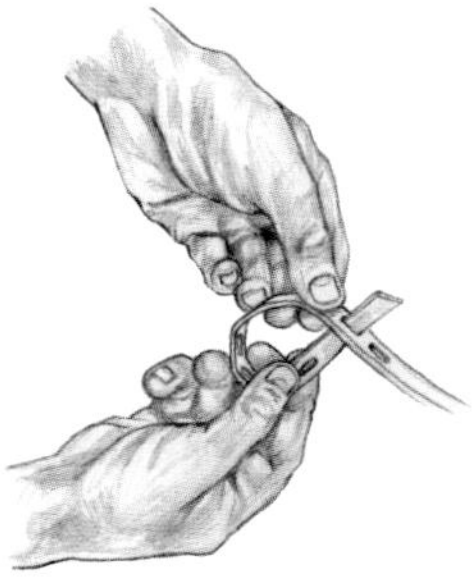

STEP 4

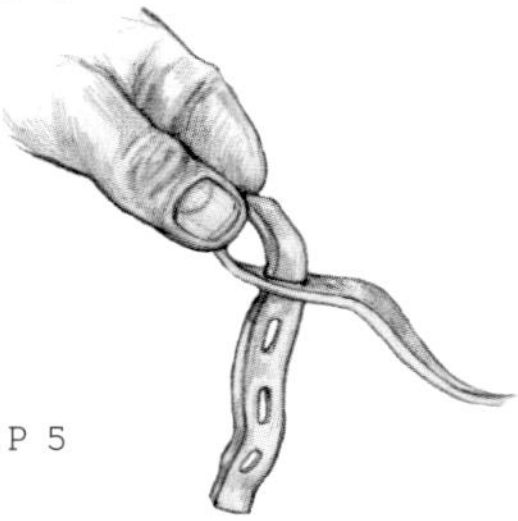

STEP 5

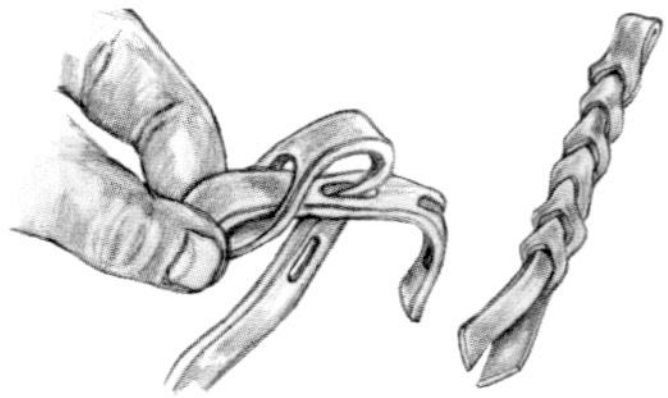

STEP 6

FACTS

A strand is one of several cords that braids and knots are made of. The term "strap" refers to the entire braid.

hole a few centimeters from the center of the strap, and then make a hole in the other half of the strap a "punch's" length farther down from the first hole. Continue to make additional holes in this alternating manner with one end's hole always a "punch's" length farther down from the other end's hole. If you have placed the holes correctly, it will not be possible to see through them when the strap is folded in half and the two halves are on top of each other.

STEP 4 Thread each end through the holes on the opposite end: Start by finding the hole closest to the middle of the strap, take the other end of the strap and insert it in the hole.

STEP 5 Now the holes are in the order in which they will be threaded with the strap's two halves. Thread the end through the next hole and repeat this until the braid is complete.

STEP 6 When the hole braid is finished, cut the ends of the strap to the desired length.

MAGIC BRAID (OR MYSTERY BRAID)

The magic braid consists of three or more strands that are not cut all the way down to the leather's ends. The leather is intact at the ends, so braiding might seem impossible. The braid is made by a combination of braiding and threading the lower end of the braid through the braid itself. The strap's width and length are important: As a general rule, the length of the braid's three strands or thongs should be about three times the total width of the strap in order to be able to do a complete braid weave. The finished magic braid usually consists of several complete braid weaves. This will become clearer later.

TOOLS AND MATERIALS

end punch
slab for punching
cardboard for pattern
strap cutter
revolving punch
rawhide mallet
slide rule
cutting mat
Stanley knife blade
stitching groover
awl

STEP 1 Make a pattern from cardboard that has the desired width and length and that includes the holes that need to be made in the leather. The holes will be placed at both ends of the knife cuts you make when you cut the braid into three strands, which helps keep the leather from splitting. A braid that has a total width of 21 mm should have parallel holes located at 7 mm intervals. The braid's three strands will each be 7 mm wide. When you determine the total width of your braid, you need to take into account the width of the buckles or buttons that you will use. You may want to make the total width of your braid be the width of the end punch you will use to cut the ends of the braid. A well thought-out pattern makes your work easier.

STEP 2 Use the pattern as a measurement guide with the strap cutter when you set it to the correct width. You should also set the strap cutter to the thickness of the leather you have chosen. A strap cutter that has been adjusted accurately cuts straps almost perfectly as long as the leather isn't soft or thinner than 1.5 mm. Start by loosening the large screw on the strap cutter. Also loosen the screws that regulate the thickness of the leather you can cut. Set the strap cutter for the thickness of your leather by tightening the screws. If the strap cutter has been used before, it may be a good idea to check to make sure the blade is sharp. Put your template in the strap cutter to set the correct width of the belt. Tighten the large screw. Now the strap cutter is ready to use.

STEP 3 Insert the leather into the strap cutter. If the blade is sharp, it will cut easily through the leather. If you need help in the beginning, you can use needle-nose pliers to grab the leather and pull until you can get a good grip with your hands. Keep in mind that the pliers will damage the leather, so use them only if you intend to cut the braid at the ends later.

STEP 4 When you have finished cutting your strap, you should mark the holes you need to make in the leather. Place the pattern on the leather and mark with the tip of an awl where the holes will be.

STEP 5 Use the smallest punch on the revolving punch to make the holes where you marked them.

STEP 6 Use an edge beveler and trim the strap's edges on both the grain and flesh sides.

MAGIC BRAID WITH 3 STRANDS

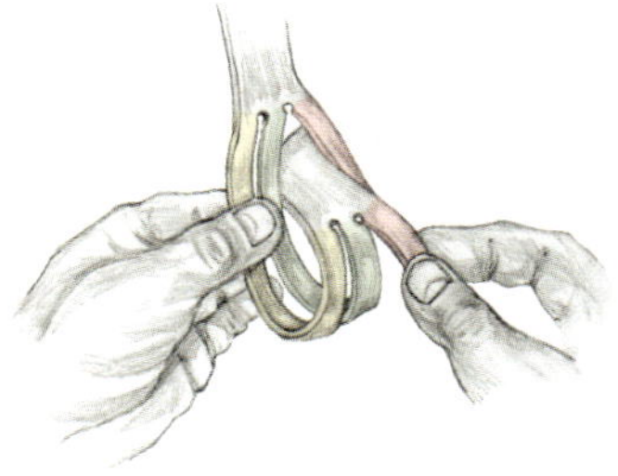

STEP 9

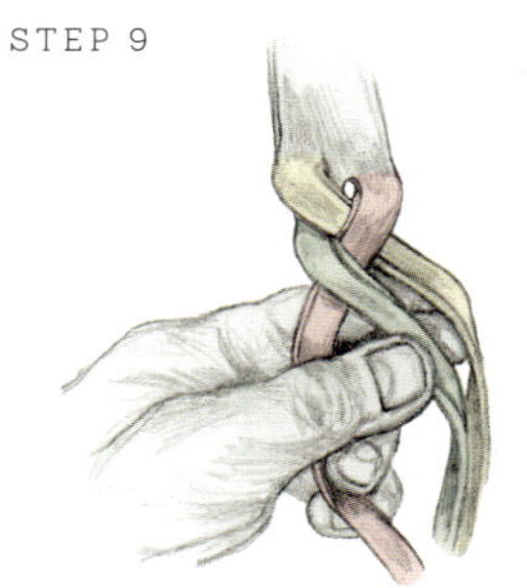

STEP 10

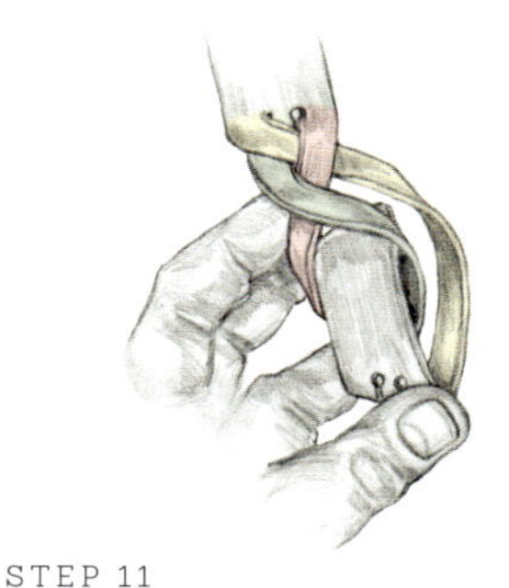

STEP 11

A BRAIDING ROTATION

MAGIC BRAID WITH 5 STRANDS

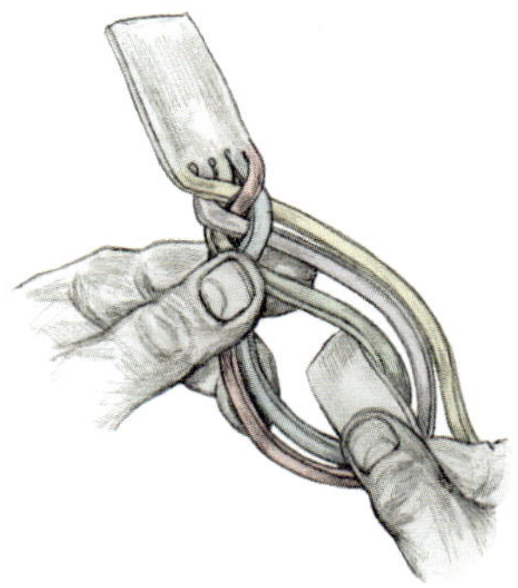

After the first braiding rotation, thread the end through the opening, either left or right of the middle strand shown in (green).

STEP 7 Use a stitching groover to mark where you are going to cut the strap to split it into three equal strands. Set the width of the stitching groover with a slide rule. The width of the individual strands of a three-stranded braid should be a third of the strap's total width. Cut identical grooves in the hair and flesh sides of the strap with the stitching groover.

STEP 8 Use a slab and a rawhide mallet along with a Stanley knife blade to make a cut in the groove you just made with the stitching groover. The blade's length is easy to shorten by breaking it off, as needed. Before hitting the back of the blade with the mallet, preferably do one last check of the proposed cut to make sure that the knife is in the groove and does not cross over the strands that have already been cut.

STEP 9 Now it is time to start braiding. The strap is now cut and divided into three strands. Strand 1 is on the left, strand 2 is in the middle and strand 3 is on the right. Start braiding by weaving the end of the belt through the opening between strand 2 and strand 3.

STEP 10 Now make three steps: lay strand 1 over strand 2; lay strand 3 over strand 1; lay strand 2 over strand 3.

STEP 11 Thread the end of the strap between strand 1 and strand 2. Now, all the strands are intertwined and the magic braid's first complete rotation is finished.

STEP 12 Repeat steps 9 through 11 until you are finished. The number of times you repeat a complete braiding rotation depends on the length of the strands you cut and the thickness of the leather you use – see below.

HOW MANY BRAIDING ROTATIONS?

For the decribed braid, each complete braiding rotation requires strands that are about 7 cm long. If the strands are cut shorter, the braid will be too tight and difficult to finish without damaging the leather. The thickness of the leather also affects the length of the braid strands. The measurement described above applies to leather up to 3 mm in thickness. If your leather is thicker, you can make the strands longer than the ones above. This is meant to be a guide. It is a matter of taste – the choice is yours!

OPTIONS: MAGIC BRAID WITH 5 STRANDS All magic braids are based on the same principle. If you have learned to make a magic braid with three strands, you can easily apply the same principle to make braids with five, seven, nine and so on. The difference is that braids with five or more strands do not begin by threading the end of the strap between the strands. The first step instead is to make as many braidings as there are strands. After that, the end of the strap is threaded through the braid. The logic of every magic braid is that, after the first braided row, the end of the strap is threaded through the braid, either to the right or left of the center strand. After the second braiding rotation or row, thread the end of the strap through the braid again, but this time on the opposite side. So if you chose to thread the end to the left of the center strand after the first row, thread it on the right side.

Imagine that the strands are numbered 1–5 from left to right: Lay strand 1 over 3; lay strand 5 over 1; lay strand 2 over 5; lay strand 4 over 2; lay strand 3 over 4. When you have done the fifth braiding rotation, you will get an opening in the braid with two strands on one side and three on the other side (see illustration on page 49). Thread the end of the strap through the braid, either to the right or left of the center strand (step 3). Now you have a messy braid. Don't worry, it fixes itself soon. Do another five braidings. Now, there will once again be an opening with two strands on one side and three on the other side. Thread the end of the strap through the opening on the opposite side of the center strand than you did before.

ROUND BRAID

A round braid is made of four or more even-numbered strands, where the outer right and outer left strands are alternately carried behind the braid and then braided between two or more strands on the opposite side. The round braid can also be braided around a core of string or leather. A core is suitable if you braid with thinner cords, 1 mm or so, because the thinner leather does not retain the round shape of the braid.

TOOLS AND MATERIALS

hobby knife
fid or sewing awl
strap cutter or ruler and rotary cutter
keyring or holster clip

STEP 1 Start by cutting the strands or cords with your strap cutter. You need two cords for every four-strand braid. Set the desired width and thickness of the strap cutter. It can be difficult to cut leather that is thinner than 1.5 mm with a strap cutter

ROUND BRAID WITH 4 STRANDS

STEP 3

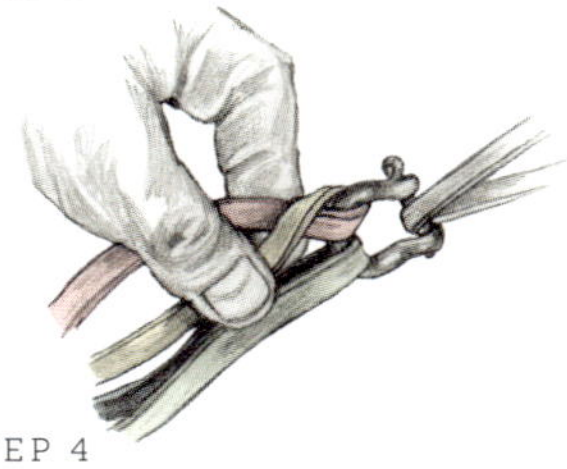

STEP 4

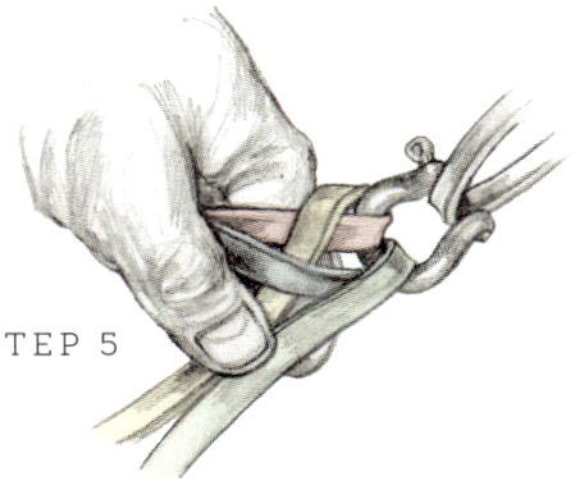

STEP 5

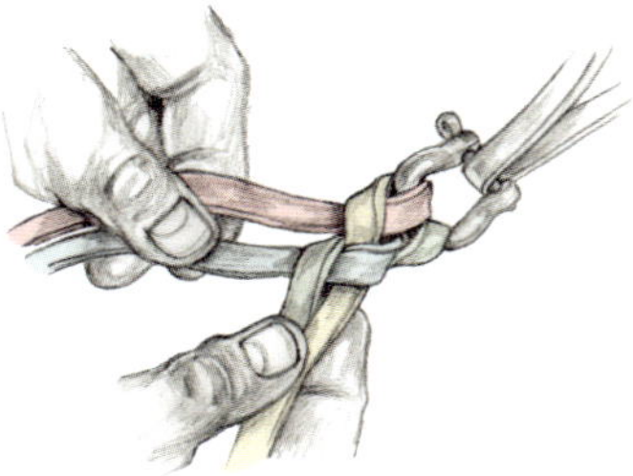

STEP 6

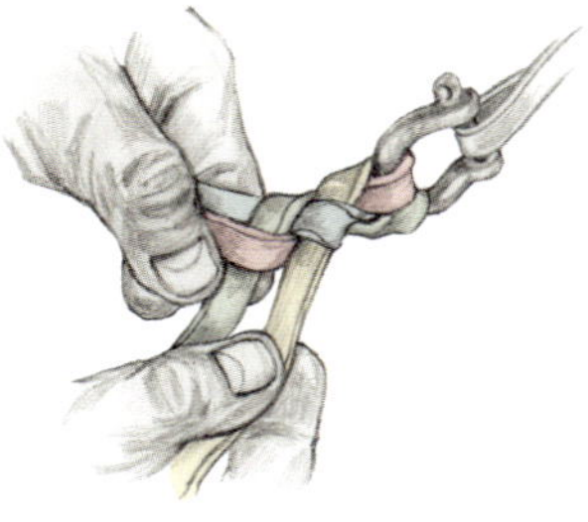

STEP 7

ROUND BRAID WITH 6 STRANDS

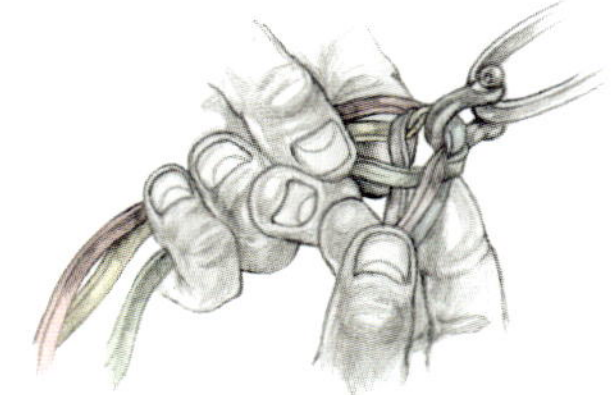

1. Cross the innermost strands in the three-strand braid's left and right side with each other.

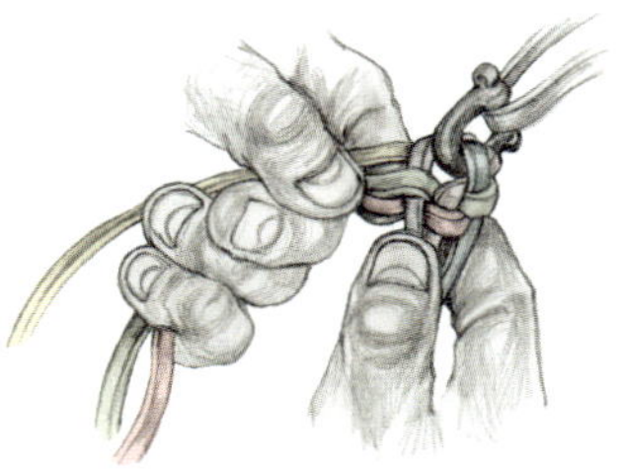

2. Take strand 1 (pink) up between the two strands on the far right. Place it over the next strand and then under the last one.

TIPS!

Whether you start braiding the outermost strand on the right or left side depends on which of the two crosses a strand when you pass it under and around the braid. The strand that is next to pass under and around the braid is always the strand that crosses a strand at the bottom of the braid. You can easily see which strand to cross if you twist the braid a half turn and look at the bottom.

if the leather is not stiff. If you're doing long braids (50 cm or more), you may need to buy a whole side of leather; the thickness should then be approximately 1.5–2 mm. Cords that are thicker than 2 mm are difficult to braid – they require dexterity and strength. Leather that is 1.5–2 mm in thickness works well for cutting into 4–6 mm wide cords. If possible, cut straps along the hide's spine where the leather is the strongest. Belly and neck leather stretches and cords lose shape when you tighten the braid. There is no exact science – again, this is only a guide.

STEP 2 After you have cut out two cords of equal length, thread them through the loop in the key ring, holster clip or other loop you want at one end of the braid. Then fasten the loop onto something to hold it in place (a wooden chair or table leg would work). You can fasten your loop to it with some knotted string. Options: To make a braid that is not attached to a ring, buckle or loop, place four cords next to each other in a bag clip or other type of clip, cross the cords as shown in illustration 1 on page 52 and braid as usual.

STEP 3 Adjust the cords so that they are of equal length on both sides of the ring. Now the two long cords become four strands that are half as long. The left side consists of a cord with the flesh side visible (strand 1) and the other with the hair side visible (strand 2). The right consists of a cord with the flesh side visible (strand 3) and one with a hair side visible (strand 4).

STEP 4 The braiding begins by turning the cord with the visible flesh side so that the narrower side is up: Turn strand 1 (yellow) clockwise for half a turn so that the hair side becomes visible, and place it over strand 2 (pink). When you do this, strand 1 crosses over on top of strand 2. Strand 2 will point southwest and strand 1 southeast.

STEP 5 Now turn strand 3 (blue) half a turn counterclockwise so that the hair side becomes visible, and place it on top of strand 1. Now, strand 2 and 3 point to the southwest and strand 1 and 4 (green) to the southeast. Now you can tighten the cords and hold strands 2 and 3 with the left hand and strands 1 and 4 with the right hand. Check that all four strands are the same length on both sides of your ring or clip.

STEP 6 Take strand 4 (on the far right) behind the braid and up between strands 2 and 3. Then put it over strand 3 to end up back on your right side in your right hand. Tighten the braid lightly!

STEP 7 Now take strand 2 (on the far left) behind the braid and up between strands 1 and 4. Then put it over strand 4 to ultimately end up on your left side in your left hand. Tighten the braid lightly! Repeat steps 6 and 7 with all four strands.

OPTION: ROUND BRAID WITH 6 STRANDS

Begin by attaching the key ring, holster clip or any loop you want to a support. Then thread three cords through the ring or loop, making sure the straps are of equal length on both sides. Put a bag clip or other kind of clip over the strands that are just behind the ring so they cannot slip out. Take the three strands without a clip on the other side of the ring and begin braiding a flat, three-strand braid that is a few centimeters long. When you're done, remove the clip and adjust the flat, three-stranded braid so that the ring is in the center of it. (To make a round, six-strand braid without a loop at the end, add six strands next to each other in a clip and cross the strands in the same way as in illustration 2 on page 51). Take three strands in your left hand and three strands in your right hand. Now cross the innermost strands of the three-strand braid on the left and right sides with each other according to illustration 1 on page 51 – the right strand should lay on top of the left strand. Take the strand on the far left (strand 1) behind and around the braid counterclockwise and up between the two strands on the far right (strands 5 and 6), then put it over strand 5 and under strand 4. Do the same with the strand on the far right (strand 6): Take it behind and around the braid clockwise and up between the two strands on the far left (strand 1 and 2), then put it over strand 2 and strand 3. As with a round four-strand braid, repeat braiding with all six strands.

OPTION: ROUND BRAID WITH 8 STRANDS

Start by attaching the key ring, holster clip or other loop you want in one end of the braid in a support. Then thread three cords through the ring or loop, making sure the straps are of equal length on both sides. Put a bag clip or other kind of clip over the strands that are just behind the ring so they cannot slip out. Take the four strands on one side of the loop, cross them as shown in illustration 1 on page 51 and braid a round, four-strand braid that is a few centimeters long. When done, remove the clip and adjust the flat, four-stranded braid so that the ring is in the center of it (To make a round, eight-strand braid without a loop at the end, add eight cords next to each other in a clip and cross the strands as shown in illustration 2 on page 52). Take four strands in your left hand and four

ROUND BRAID WITH 8 STRANDS

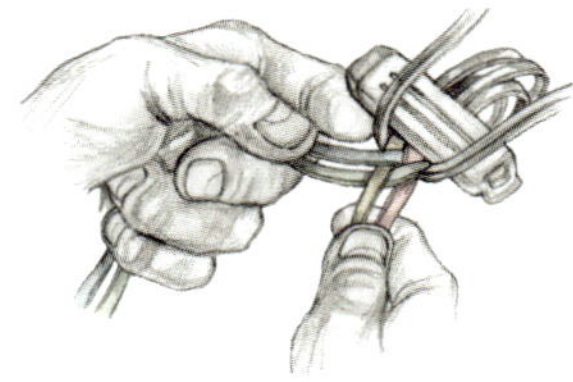

1. Cross the strands and make a round four-strand braid.

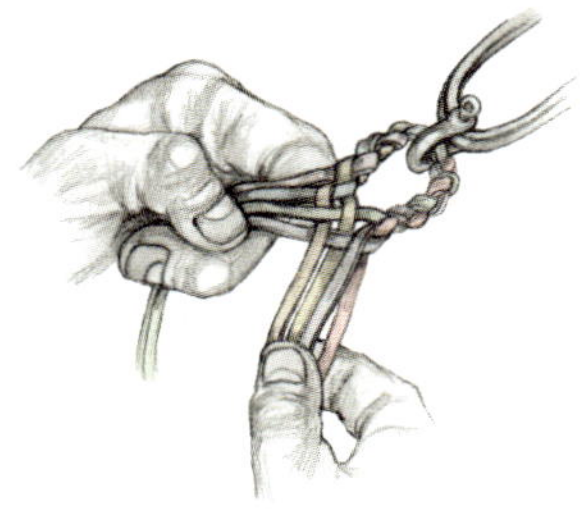

2. Cross two of the strands in the four-strand braid on the left and right sides with each other. Now you can make a round eight-strand braid.

TIPS!

The round eight-strand braid can be intertwined in a herringbone pattern by bringing each strand between the two middle strands, i.e., under the two strands, over the two strands.

TURK'S HEAD KNOT

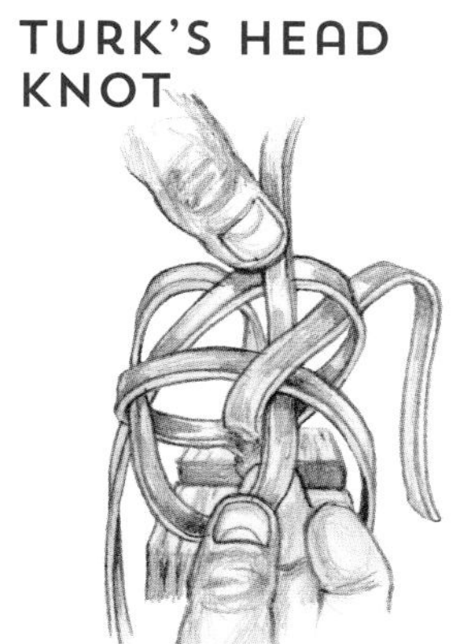

STEP 2

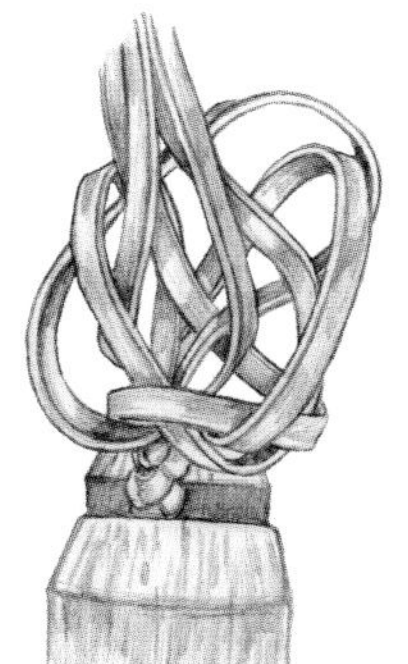

STEP 3

FINISHED KNOT

strands in your right hand. Now cross two of the strands in each hand with each other as shown in illustration 2 on page 52. Braid according to the same technique used for all round braids: Take the strand on the far left (strand 1) behind the braid counterclockwise and up between the two strands on the far right (strands 7 and 8), then lay it over strand 7, under strand 6 and over strand 5. Do the same with the strand on the far right (strand 8). Repeat braiding with all eight strands.

»——→ FINISHING ROUND BRAIDS

When you finish your braid, it is time to secure it. Which type of fastening you choose depends on what the braid will be used for, but whichever it will be, it is best to tie a string around the braid so that it does not unravel. A waxed thread is easy to knot. In the various steps I describe for Turk's head and gaucho knots, the idea is that every step should be repeated for all strands. There are several ways to end a braid; here are some suggestions for two knots, one easier and one more difficult.

TURK'S HEAD OR PINEAPPLE KNOT

A Turk's head or pineapple knot is an easy knot that you can put on a braided key ring, for example. As with braiding, all knots are done by repeating the same steps. The steps described will be done exactly the same with all the strands. In the example below, the Turk's head knot is tied like the end of a braid with four strands, which means you should repeat each part four times. The same knot can be made with six or eight strands, and all steps are to be repeated six or eight times, respectively.

STEP 1 Start the Turk's head knot by making an end knot according to the illustrated instructions on page 54. Do not tighten the end knot!

STEP 2 Take each strand to the right and put it around the strand coming from the braid and then up through the end knot's opening so that it comes out at the top of the knot. Repeat with all strands.

STEP 3 Tighten the knot. To keep the knot symmetrical, it is important that all strands be tightened equally and that this be done in stages – use the awl tool for this. Pull the knot in stages where all four strands are tightened one by one, beginning with the closest strand coming out of the braid. When you have pulled on all four strands, select a point further "forward" in the knot. All strands pass through the knot exactly the same so you can track the strands through the knot and tighten them. The last tightening you do in each strand is the one that sticks out from the top of the knot. You will probably need to do this a number of times. Just make sure you have pulled the same amount for each strand. When the knot begins to tighten, it is more difficult to correct any unevenness that results from not tightening in stages.

ROUND KNOT AND BUTTON, GAUCHO KNOT AND BUTTON

The round knot and gaucho knot begin and end in exactly the same way. The difference is that in the round knot the strands are braided only half a rotation, while in the gaucho knot they are braided one full turn. The round knot is the simpler of the two. But it's worth your while to learn both, because they provide a wider range of options than the Turk's head knot. Both can be braided with 4, 6 and 8 strands. The instructions provided on page 55 describe making knots using four strands, but the approach is the same regardless of the number of strands. Start with four, because it is easier to keep track of the strands.

ROUND BUTTON AND GAUCHO BUTTON If you want to make smaller buttons completely out of leather for leather projects or an article of clothing, then the round button or gaucho button are perfect. The size of the finished button is determined by the number of strands and the width and thickness of the strands. Kangaroo leather is suitable for buttons as it produces a cord that can withstand being pulled without breaking. A width of 3 mm and a thickness of 1 mm is suitable. To make a button with four strands, begin by threading the two cords through a ring (for example, a large paper clip) or a smaller shackle. It is important that the ring or shackle can be removed when the button is complete, because the strands that sit around the ring or shackle will form two loops that you use to attach the button to your leather item or clothing. When you have threaded the strands through the ring, tie a string, preferably waxed, a few times around all the strands. Wrap the string around so that it covers about 7 mm of the strands above the ring or shackle. Then make an end knot. Follow the instructions below to make the a round knot or a gaucho knot.

ROUND KNOT AND GAUCHO KNOT I use both round knots and gaucho knots for the finishing of braids. It could be

HOW TO MAKE AN END KNOT

1. Take strand 1 (yellow) and place it between strand 2 (green) and strand 3 (blue).

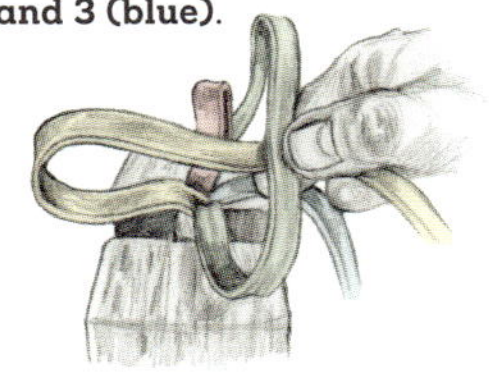

2. Place strand 2 on top of strand 1 and between strands 3 and 4.

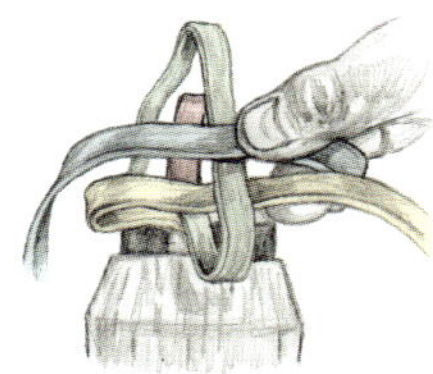

3. Place strand 3 on top of strand 2 and between strands 4 and 1.

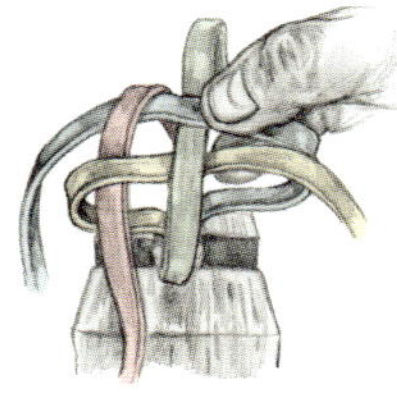

4. Place strand 4 on top of strand 3 and then under strand 1.

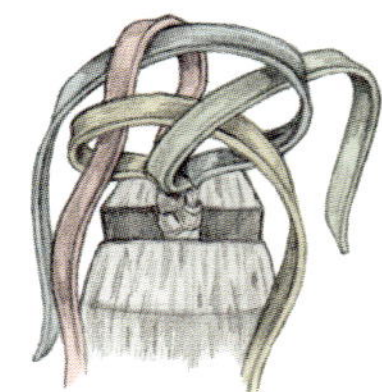

5. Tighten the end knot if you are going to continue with a gaucho knot, or leave it loose for a Turk's head knot.

GAUCHO KNOT STEP-BY-STEP

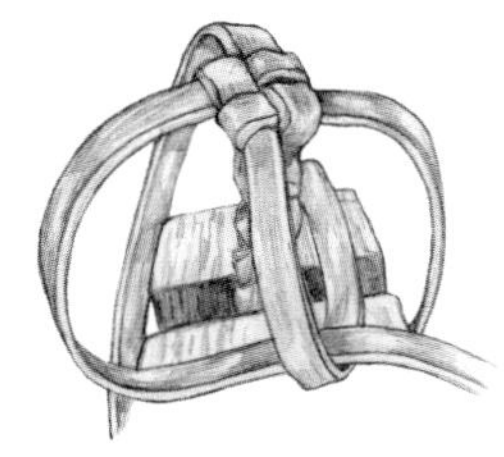

STEP 3.1

STEP 3.2

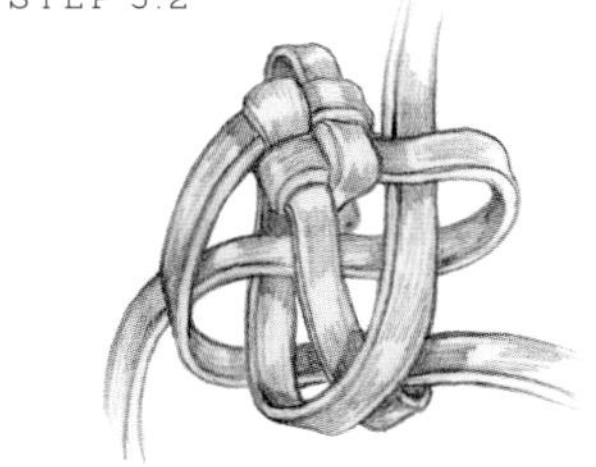

STEP 4.1

STEP 4.2

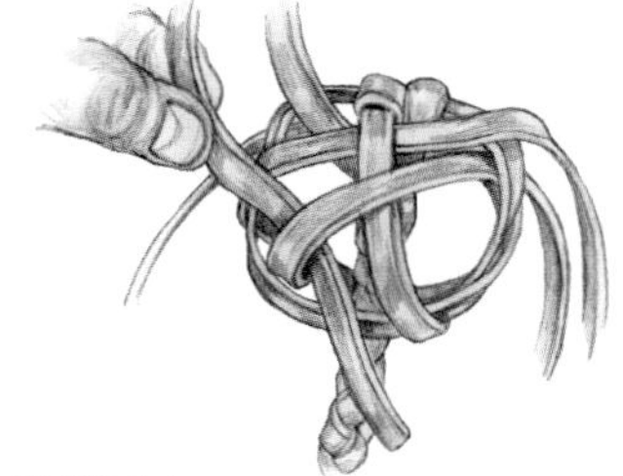

STEP 5.1

a knot at the end of a braided key ring or perhaps a knot that serves as a button in a braided bracelet. For the gaucho knot in the braid made in the keychain project (page 86), I have used four cords that are 5–6 mm wide, and 1.5–2 mm thick. For the round knot on the braided bracelet (page 97), I have used four kangaroo leather cords that are 3 mm wide and 1 mm thick. The gaucho knot with the wider and thicker straps will be about 3–4 cm in diameter, depending on how hard you tighten it. The round knot with the 3 mm wide laces is about 10–12 mm and has a core of wood or leather. The gaucho knot may need a core so as not to lose shape when you tighten it. When I've braided gaucho knots with thinner cords, I have used wooden balls from a hobby shop or self-made cores of thicker leather (about 5 mm), which I cut to the correct diameter with a larger (7–10 mm) round punch. With the wooden balls, I drilled the hole so that it is less than the braid's diameter, but large enough for all the strands to be threaded through it. I use a revolving punch to make the holes in leather cores.

STEP 1 When you are finished braiding, tie a waxed linen thread around the braid so that it does not unravel. If your gaucho knot needs a core (see above), start by threading the braid's strands through the core. Note! The simpler round knot usually does not need a core.

STEP 2 Make an end knot at the top of the braid and tighten it. Be sure that it is tightened symmetrically since the end knot will appear at the top of the finished gaucho knot.

STEP 3 Take each strand and place it under the strand to the left. The fourth strand will be just like the other, placed under the one on the left, and then over the next strand on the right and up through the loop that has been formed.

STEP 4 Now place each strand over the first strand to the right and then under the next strand to the right. The ends of all four strands should now come out through the top of the knot. If you are braiding a round knot, end the knot by going to Step 7 and Step 8.

STEP 5 If you are braiding a gaucho knot, all four strands will continue in the counter-clockwise direction going downward in the knot: Place each strand over the closest one to the right, then under the next strand that sits slightly below the right and finally over the last strand at the bottom. When you repeat this with all four strands, the strands should come out of the knot's underside and point downward.

STEP 6 Now each strand passes up through the knot counterclockwise and comes out through the top of the knot. Place each strand first under the bottom strand. Continue diagonally upward to the right by passing above the two strands to finally pass under the two strands forming a cross nearest to the end knot on the knot's top side. Repeat this step with all four strands. Now all four strands should come out through the top of the knot next to the end knot.

STEP 7 Before the knot is tightened, all four sides must pass through the center of the braid and out through the bottom of the knot. Place each strand over the strand to the right that comes from the end knot on the top side, and thread it down into the gap and finally out through the opening at the bottom of the knot. Now the knot is finished. Before tightening the strands, it is important that you check that it is symmetrical.

STEP 8 When you tighten the gaucho knot, it is important that you do it in stages. Follow the instructions for a Turk's head knot in step 3. When the knot is fully tightened, trim the ends of the strands that stick out.

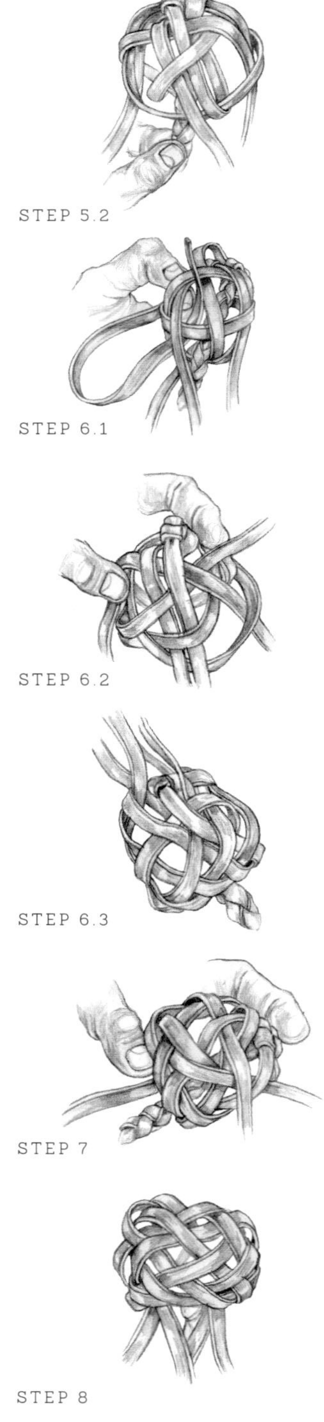

STEP 5.2

STEP 6.1

STEP 6.2

STEP 6.3

STEP 7

STEP 8

Part four

PROJECTS

Now is the time to use your newly acquired knowledge. These projects are of varying difficulty, and all the techniques used in each project are referred to in part two. If you have read and practiced, none of the projects should be terribly difficult; some will just take more time than others. Patience is the key to a successful result. Good luck!

KEY HOLDER / WALLET CHAIN

TWO VARIANTS OF A SIMPLE HOLE BRAID

MATERIALS

- 2 leather straps for key holder, 35 cm × 15 mm, 1.5 mm thick
- 2 leather straps for wallet chain, 60 cm × 15 mm, 1.5 mm thick

TOOLS

- oblong punch, 12–15 mm
- slab for punching/striking
- burnisher (optional)
- canvas cloth
- edge beveler
- contact adhesive and brush
- leather
- grease
- roller
- polishing liquid
- strap cutter or ruler and rotary cutter
- eraser
- rawhide mallet
- wooden creaser or creasing iron
- slide rule
- cutting mat
- awl

STEP 1 Use a strap cutter to cut two leather straps according to the specified dimensions (image a). The width of the finished strap will actually be 10 mm, but, in order to be able to trim off any adhesive residue on the strap edges, it should be slightly wider at the beginning: 15 mm.

STEP 2 Apply contact adhesive onto the flesh side of both straps according to the instruction on page 28. When the glue has dried (water-based adhesive should be slightly sticky, solvent-based adhesive should be completely dry), press the two sides together. Be sure to place the straps edge to edge. Use a roller to press them together (image b). Now you have a 15 mm wide and 3 mm thick leather strap with the hair side on both sides.

STEP 3 Use the strap cutter to cut the glued strap to 10 mm in width (image c). You should cut off about 2.5 mm from each side. The beauty of cutting the strap to the correct width after gluing is that you get the edges completely free of glue. If you accidentally get glue on the hair side, you can wipe it off with a piece of eraser.

STEP 4 If you want to decorate the edge of the strap, you can use a wooden creaser or creasing iron (see page 38).

STEP 5 Trim the edges of the strap (image d) and burnish it according to the instructions on page 39.

STEP 6 If you want to rub leather grease into the braid, it would be best do this before you make the holes and braid the strap. This way, leather grease won't get into the braid holes.

STEP 7 Make holes in the strap with an oblong punch. For a strap that's 10 mm wide and 3 mm thick you need a punch that is about 12–15 mm. Fold the strap in half and decide how big the loop for the key ring or other fastener should be. If the loop is to be 6 cm, make the first hole 3 cm from the strap's midpoint. Then make a second hole in the other half, placing it 3 cm plus a punch length farther down from the first hole. Continue to make two more holes on each half of the strap with a punch length's distance between the holes (image e). Overall, there should be six holes alternately placed so that you cannot see through them when the strap is folded in half and the two halves are on top of each other (image f). If you're making a wallet chain, fold the strap at each end, instead of the center, about 10–12 cm at each end.

STEP 8 Put your key ring or fastener in the middle of the strap and make a hole braid according to the instructions on page 46. Finish by cutting the ends to the desired length. If you're making a wallet chain, you will braid both ends of the strap using the same technique. You will need to attach a fastener when the braiding is complete.

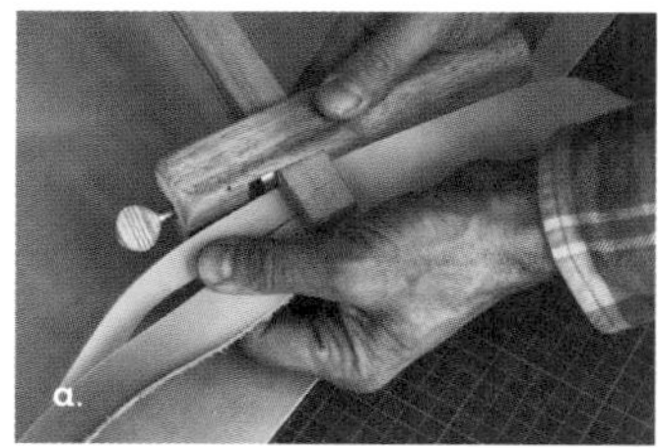
a.

b.

c.

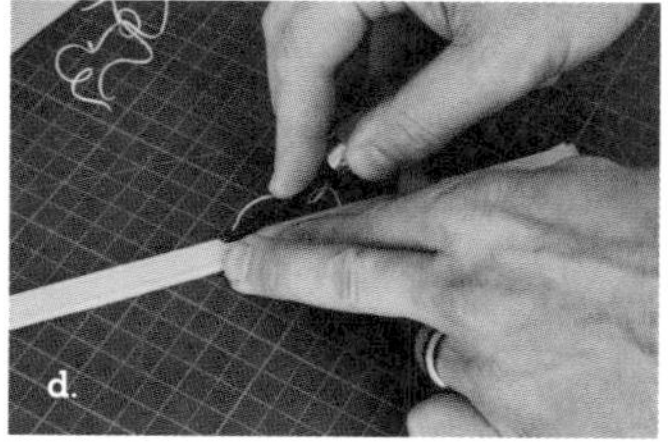
d.

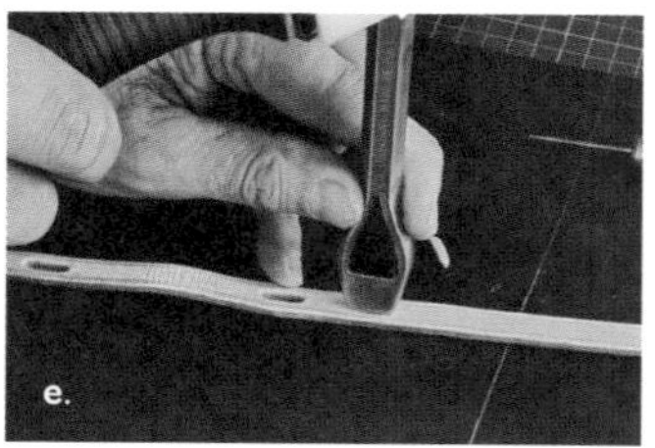
e.

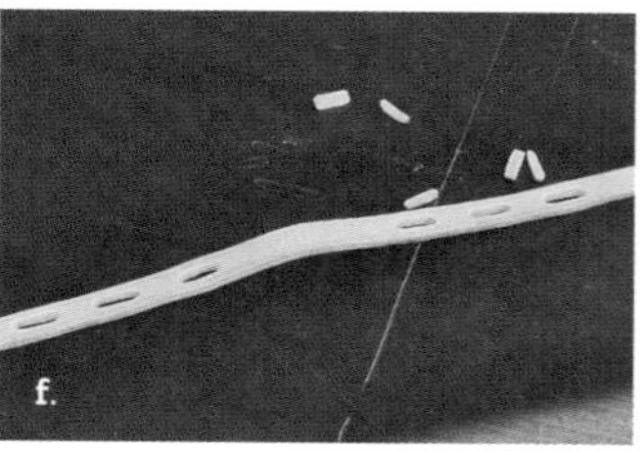
f.

BRAIDED BRACELET

WITH TOGGLE CLASP

MATERIALS

1 leather strap, 25 cm × 21 mm, 3 mm thick
1 toggle clasp, 21 mm wide
cardboard, white paper and glue for the pattern

TOOLS

oblong punch, 12 mm
pricking iron
slab for punching/striking
beveler, 1mm wide
ruler
leather grease
needle and thread for saddle stitching
strap cutter
revolving punch
rotary cutter
rawhide mallet
stitching pony
slide rule
cutting mat
awl
stitching groover
U-shaped end punch, 21 mm
Stanley knife blade

STEP 1 Start by making a pattern. Use a U-shaped end punch with a width of 21 mm as a guide. The pattern will be 21 mm wide and about 25 cm long. Because the strap is 21 mm wide and the braid has three strands, each strand will be 7 mm wide. The length of the strands is 14 cm. To divide the pattern into three equally wide strands, make two holes in the pattern 7 mm from the edge. Holes should be located at both ends of each strand for a total of four holes, two holes 14 cm apart at each end (image a).

STEP 2 Set the strap cutter to the width of the pattern and the thickness of the leather. If necessary, use a ruler and a rotary cutter to make a straight edge on the leather. Cut out your strap with the strap cutter.

STEP 3 Place the pattern on your strap and use an awl to mark where to make the holes in the leather.

STEP 4 Make the holes with the smallest punch of the revolving punch on top of the marks you made with the awl. The purpose of making holes in the end of each of the strands is to prevent the leather from splitting when it is braided.

STEP 5 Trim the edge of the strap on both the hair and flesh sides.

STEP 6 To mark where you will cut to get three strands of the exact same width, set the stitching groover to 7 mm using a slide rule. Then cut a groove between the holes on both the hair and flesh sides (image b).

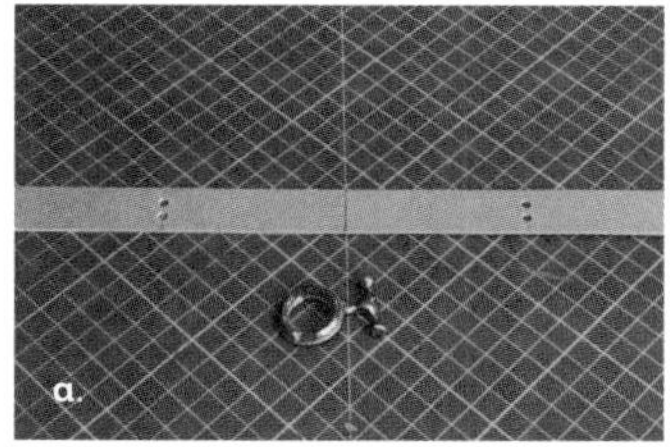
a.

b.

c.

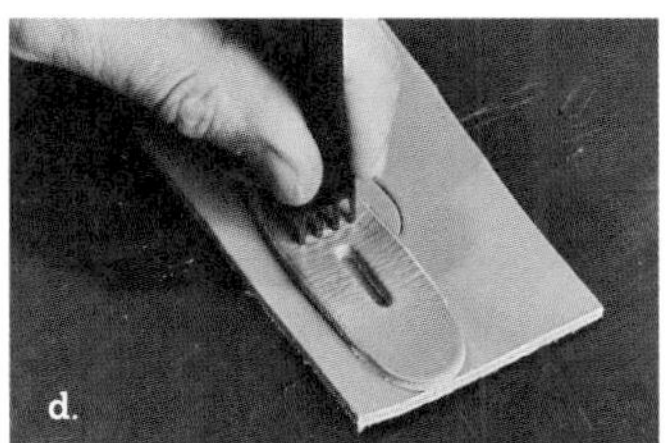
d.

e.

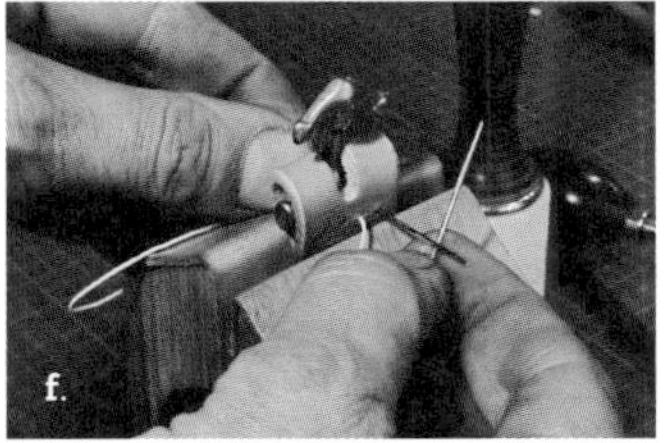
f.

STEP 7 Use the knife blade and mallet to cut out the strands. Insert the blade into the groove you made with the stitching groover and carefully tap with the mallet until the blade cuts through the leather. Do the same in the second groove.

STEP 8 Rub leather grease on both sides of the strap.

STEP 9 Braid the strands according to the instructions for a magic braid with three strands on page 47.

STEP 10 Measure the length you want for your bracelet so you know where to put the clasp. Make a hole with a 12 mm oblong punch at both ends where the clasp will be attached.

STEP 11 When you know the length you want, cut the ends of the strap with a U-shaped end punch. Leave 2 cm at the ends beyond the oblong hole to fold around the clasp and for seam allowance (image c).

STEP 12 Make stitching holes with a pricking iron to mark where you want to sew. Prick the holes on top first, then fold the leather around the clasp and mark it again in the same holes (image d and e).

STEP 13 Set in the clasp and sew according to the instructions on page 35 (image f).

BRACELET WITH SILVER BUTTON

AND ROUND BRAIDED CLASP

MATERIALS

1 leather strap,
 25 cm × 20 mm, 3 mm thick
1 clasp, snap or button
cardboard, white paper and glue for the pattern

TOOLS

slab for punching/striking
edge beveler, 1 mm wide
ruler
leather grease
strap cutter
clean, white cotton cloth or white canvas cloth
revolving punch
rotary cutter
rawhide mallet
slide rule
cutting mat
awl
stitching groover
U-shaped end punch, 21 mm wide or slightly wider
Stanley knife blade

STEP 1 Start by making a pattern. Use a U-shaped end punch, with a width of 21 mm, as a guide. The pattern will be 20 mm wide and 25 cm long, depending on the clasp you choose. Because the braid has five strands, each strand will be 4 mm wide. The length of the strands should be 14 cm. To divide the pattern into five strands of equal width, make four holes 4 mm apart on the pattern (image a). The holes will be located at both ends of each strand. In total, there should be eight holes at 14 cm intervals.

STEP 2 Set the strap cutter to the width of the pattern and the thickness of the leather. If necessary, use a ruler and a rotary cutter to prepare a straight edge on the leather. Cut your strap.

STEP 3 Place the pattern on your strap and make holes in the leather with an awl (image b). Even the smallest punch of the revolving punch is too big for this.

STEP 4 Trim the edges of the strap on both the hair and flesh sides with an edge beveler.

STEP 5 To mark where to cut to get five strands of equal width, first set the stitching groover to 4 mm using the slide rule. Next, cut a groove between the holes closest to the edges of both the hair and flesh sides. Then set the stitching groover to 8 mm and cut a groove between the holes farthest in from the edges of both hair and flesh sides (image c).

STEP 6 Use the knife blade and mallet to cut out the strands: Insert the blade into the groove you made with the stitching groover and carefully tap the back of the blade with the mallet until it cuts through the leather (image d). Do the same in all four grooves.

STEP 7 Rub leather grease on both sides.

STEP 8 Braid the strands according to the instructions for a magic braid with five strands on page 49 (image e).

STEP 9 If you want to get some patina on the braid right away, you can rub in leather grease with a clean, white canvas cloth. Apply firm pressure over the braid. Do not use too much grease as it can easily settle into the braid's intertwining folds.

STEP 10 Determine the length the bracelet will be – it depends on the clasp you choose. With a snap, the bracelet needs to overlap about 3–4 cm, so use the wrist measurement plus 3–4 cm. The clasp I chose (shown in the picture on the previous page) is a fine silver button I managed to buy online. I cut the bracelet with a U-shaped end punch that is slightly wider than the strap. Then I sewed on the button with a waxed synthetic thread, and at the other end I made four holes with the smallest punch of a revolving punch. For a loop, I braided a round four-strand braid (see page 50) from leather cords 3 mm wide and 1 mm thick (image f). At each end, I made a Turk's head knot to secure it, as described on page 53. I made a Turk's head knot at one end first, then I threaded the braid through the four holes and finished with a Turk's head knot on the other end. Done!

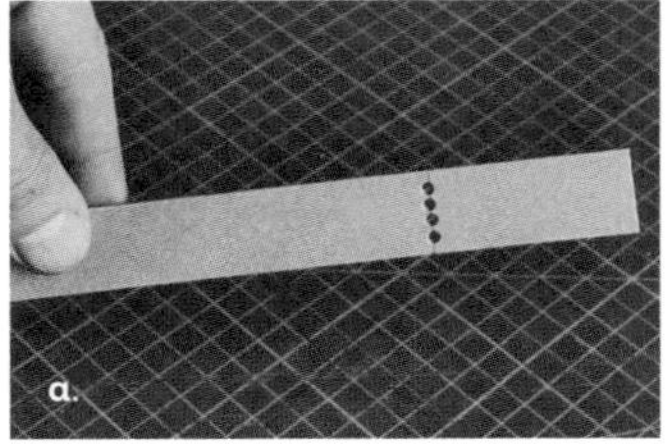

a.

b.

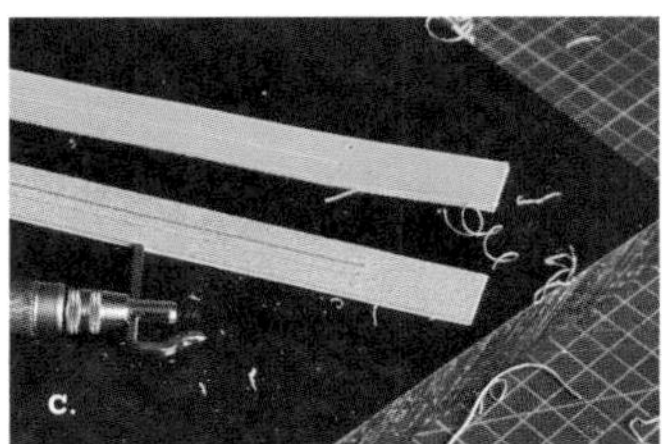

c.

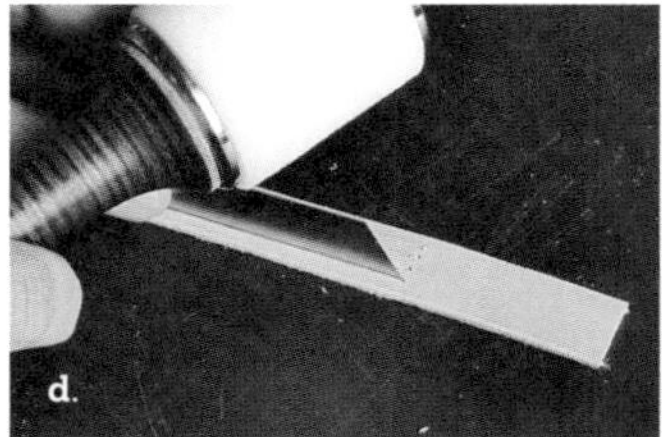

d.

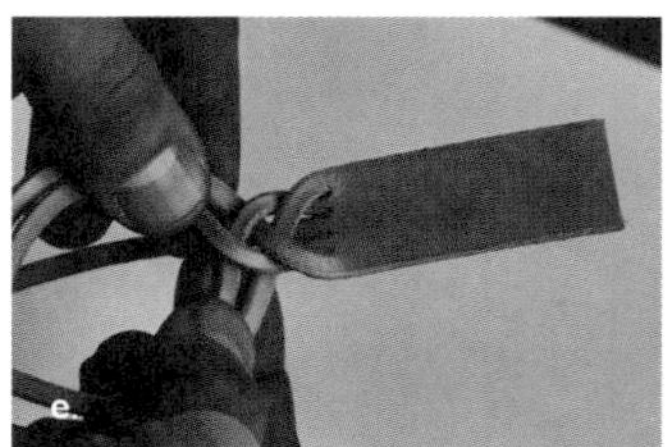

e.

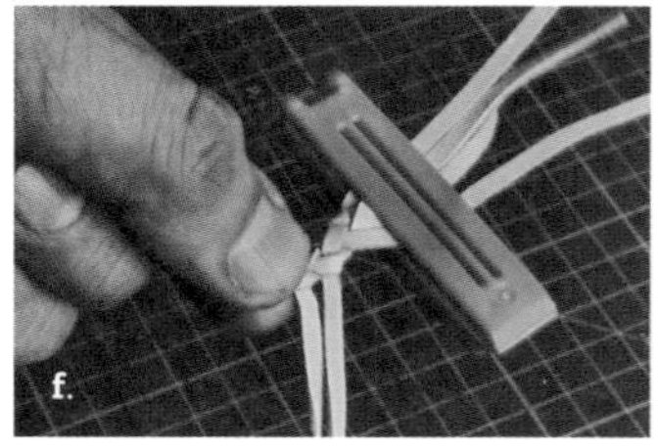

f.

CARD CASE

WITH POCKETS FOR MONEY AND CREDIT CARDS

MATERIALS

4 leather pieces, 7 × 10 cm, 1–1.5 mm thick
cardboard, white paper and glue for the pattern

TOOLS

pricking iron
hobby knife or end punch for round corners
slab for punching/striking
burnisher or canvas cloth
edge beveler
contact adhesive and brush
saddler's scratch or compass or slide rule
nail file or sandpaper
needle and thread for saddle stitching
burnishing fluid
rotary cutter
gum eraser
rawhide mallet wooden creaser or creasing iron
stitching pony
cutting mat
awl

STEP 1 Start by making the patterns: You need a rectangular pattern with four straight sides for the two center pieces, and a rectangular pattern with a self-designed upper edge for the two outer card pockets. I chose to make the pockets with a partially curved edge. Draw your patterns on paper first, using your credit card as a reference point. Standard dimensions of credit cards are approximately 5.4 × 8.5 cm, but you will make your credit card holder about 1.5 cm wider and higher (7 × 10 cm) to have extra room for sewing and to keep the card from falling out of the case. Cut out your patterns: Use a rotary cutter and a ruler for the straight edges and a hobby knife to cut the round corners (image a). Glue the patterns onto cardboard, allow them to dry and then cut them out from the cardboard.

STEP 2 Mark your patterns with a sharp awl on the leather, and cut out the leather pieces using a rotary cutter on the straight lines and a hobby knife for the corners. If you have an end punch for rounded corners, that works best.

STEP 3 Make decorative lines with a wooden creaser or creasing iron along the upper edge on all four pieces of leather (image b) – make one line 3 mm from the edge and another line 6 mm from the edge.

STEP 4 Trim the edges and then round off the upper edge on all four pieces with a nail file or sandpaper to prepare it for burnishing.

STEP 5 Burnish the upper edge of each piece according to the instructions on page 39.

STEP 6 Apply a 5 mm wide bead of adhesive along the edges of the back of the two pieces that will sit in the middle of the card holder, but keep the top edge free of glue (image c). When the glue has dried (again, when using water-based adhesive it should be slightly sticky), press the two sides together. Be sure to put them edge to edge. Press gently along the edges with a roller.

STEP 7 Glue both of the outer pockets in place. Begin by placing them precisely on top of the inner piece of leather. In order to know how far up you need to glue, use an awl to make a mark on the inner leather piece where the outer edge of the pocket ends (image d). Do this on both sides.

STEP 8 With a nail file, roughen up the shiny surface of the inner piece of the hair side up to the mark you made with the awl. Apply a 5 mm wide bead of glue where you have filed on the hair side and another equal amount of glue onto the outer pocket's back (image e). When the glue is dry, press the two outer pockets to the inner pieces. Press it all together with a roller.

STEP 9 Prepare the three edges that have not yet been burnished by trimming them and sanding them with a nail file. Sand the edges and corners smooth to round off the edges. The more energy you spend on getting even and rounded edges, the better the result will be after burnishing.

STEP 10 Before burnishing, mark where you are going to make your seam with the pricking iron. I made my mark 3–4 mm from the edge. You can use a compass or a slide rule to make the mark. Then use a pricking iron and rawhide mallet to make holes along the marked line (image f). To go around the corners, it's easier if you use a pricking iron with two teeth.

STEP 11 Sew along the sides of the credit card pocket and the lower edge according to the instructions on page 35.

STEP 12 Finish by burnishing the edges.

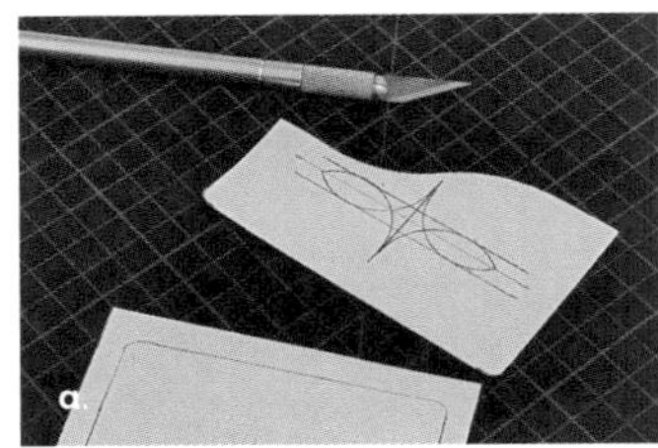
a.

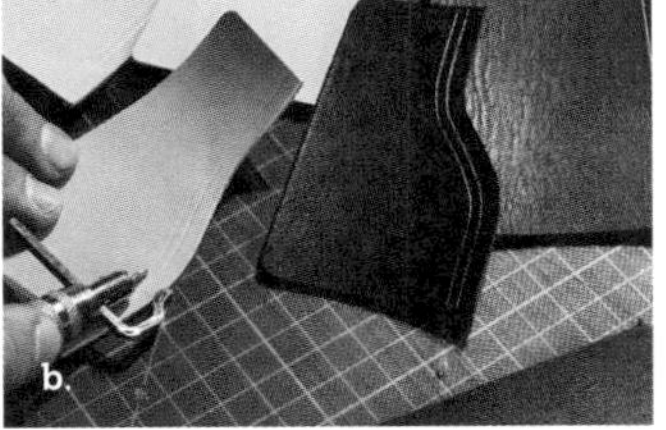
b.

c.

d.

e.

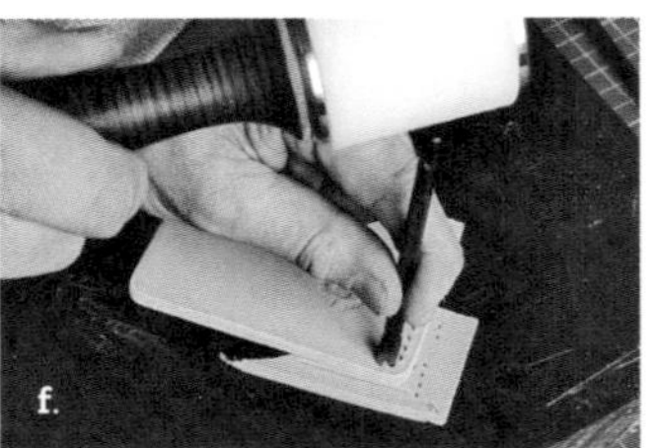
f.

10
Skatteverket
UTFÄRDARE
170 CM
INNEHAVARENS NAMNTECKNING
LONE WOLF

CELL PHONE CASE

SIMPLE STYLE WITH THUMB GRIP

MATERIALS

2 leather pieces = 2–2.5 cm wider and 1–1.25 cm longer than the cell phone's measurement. The leather should be about 1–1.5 mm thick.
cardboard, white paper, and glue for the pattern
1 mold in wood or plastic

TOOLS

pricking iron
hobby knife or end punch for round corners
slab for punching / striking
burnisher or canvas cloth
edge beveler
contact adhesive and brush
ruler or slide rule
nail file or sandpaper
needle and thread for saddle stitching
saddler's scratch or compass
burnishing fluid
rotary cutter
gum eraser
rawhide mallet stitching pony
cutting mat
awl
U-shaped end punch

STEP 1 Begin by cutting out a mold that has the same dimensions as your cell phone from a plastic or wood cutting board. Cheap cutting boards are available in most department stores, and sometimes you can even find boards with approximately the same thickness as the cell phone.

STEP 2 Draw a pattern on paper, using the same measurements as your cell phone but with an extra margin added to the width and length (see Materials). For thinner cell phones, such as an iphone, it is enough to add 2 cm to the width and 1 cm to the length. For slightly thicker phones, such as the iPhone 4 or 5, you need to add a few extra mm. The pattern should also be a few mm narrower at the bottom, otherwise, the case will look like a pair of flared trousers. Cut out the sketched pattern, glue it onto cardboard, and cut out the cardboard when the glue is dry (image a).

STEP 3 Use a sharp awl to mark the leather using your pattern and cut out the leather pieces. Use a rotary cutter and ruler for the straight lines and cut out the circular recesses on the case's sides with the U-shaped end punch (image b). Round off the corners at the bottom with an end punch designed for corners (image c).

STEG 4 File or sand about 5 mm from the edge along the sides of the case with a nail or sandpaper and then apply glue to the surface (image d). When the glue is still slightly sticky, press the two halves together. Be sure to put them edge to edge. Press it together with a roller.

STEP 5 Even up the edges and sand away glue residue with a coarser sandpaper. Trim the edges of the case.

STEP 6 Wet the glued case in lukewarm water and slide the plastic mold down inside the case (image e). You can help shape the leather by rubbing along the edges with a glass slicker. Wet leather gets marked up easily, so work on a flat surface. Once you have shaped the leather as you want it, allow it to dry for about a day with the plastic mold inside. In order to avoid discoloration from the surface underneath, it is best to set it on a piece of plastic.

STEP 7 When the case is dry, clean any glue residue off the edges with a piece of eraser and file the edges evenly with a nail file. Then burnish the edges according to the instructions on page 39.

STEP 8 Using a compass, mark where you are going to stitch along the sides of the case (image f). Make stitch holes with the pricking iron and finish by sewing according to the instructions on page 35.

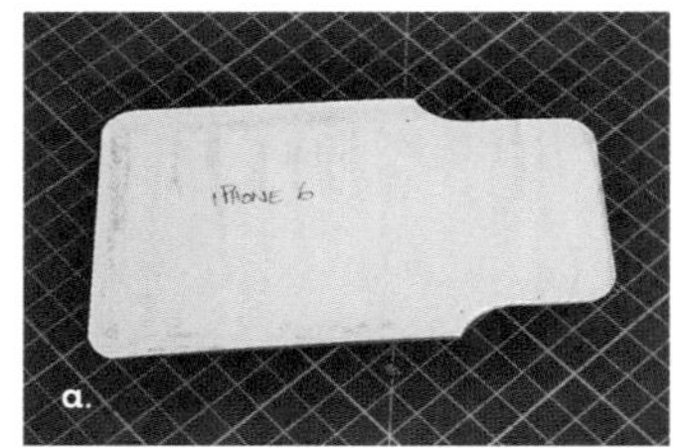
a.

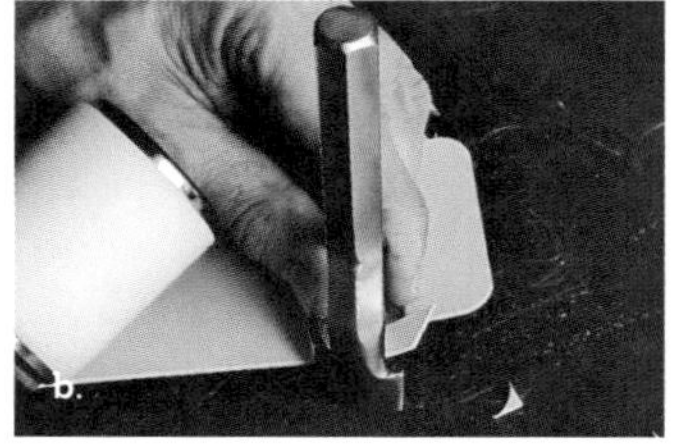
b.

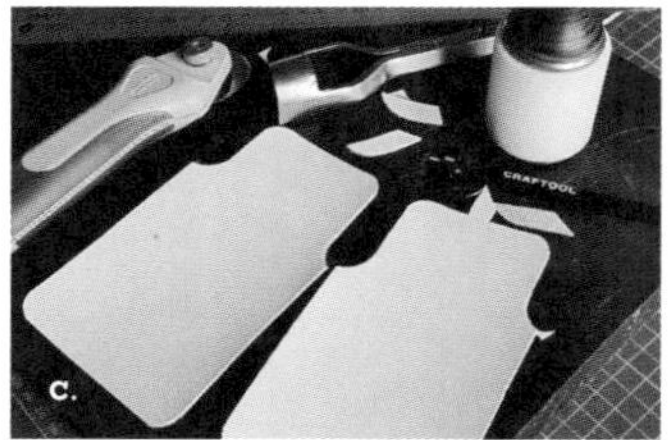
c.

d.

e.

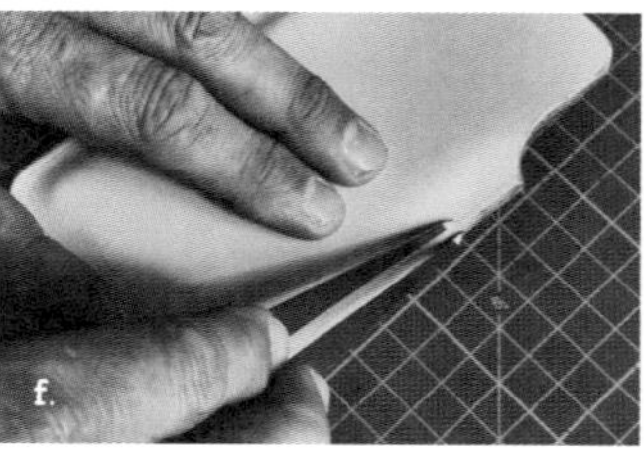
f.

KEY HOLDER FOR BELT

WITH MAGIC BRAID AND BUTTON STUDS

MATERIALS

- 1 leather strap, 35 cm × 21 mm, 3 mm thick
- 1 fastener = 22 mm
- cardboard, white paper, and glue for the pattern
- 2 button studs

TOOLS

- English point end punch, 22 mm
- pricking iron
- slab for punching/striking
- edge beveler, 1 mm
- leather grease
- needle and thread for saddle stitch
- keyhole-shaped punch
- strap cutter
- revolving punch
- slide rule or ruler
- rawhide mallet
- cutting mat
- stitching groover
- U-shaped end punch, 22 mm
- Stanley knife blade

STEP 1 The clasp for this project will have a loop that is 22 mm wide. Make a pattern from cardboard that is slightly narrower: 21 mm wide and 35 cm long. Beginning 7 cm from one end of the pattern, draw two parallel lines that are 7 cm long and have 7 mm spacing. At both ends of each line, make a hole with the smallest punch of the revolving punch.

STEP 2 Set the strap cutter to the width of the pattern and the thickness of the leather, and cut out your strap.

STEP 3 Place the pattern on your strap and mark with an awl where you are going to make the holes in the leather.

STEP 4 Make holes in the leather where you made the marks with the awl using the smallest punch of the revolving punch. The purpose of making holes at the end of each strand is to prevent the leather from splitting when it is braided.

STEP 5 To mark where to cut in order to get three strands of the exact same width, set the stitching groover at 7 mm using the slide rule. Then cut a groove between the holes on both the hair and flesh sides.

STEP 6 Trim the edges of the strap on both the hair and flesh side with an edge beveler.

STEP 7 Use the knife blade and mallet to cut out the lines; place the knife blade in the groove you made with the stitch groover and tap the mallet carefully until the blade has cut through the leather. Do the same in the second groove.

STEP 8 Rub leather grease into the strap on both sides.

STEP 9 Braid the strands according to the instructions for a magic braid with three strands on page 47.

STEP 10 Cut off the end of the strap that will be visible on the front of the key holder about 7 cm below the braid (image a). Use a 22 mm wide end punch with an English point or the blade of the Stanley knife. Mark the center of the leather strap with a slide rule or ruler so that you get the tip in the middle.

STEP 11 Cut off the other end of the strap with a U-shaped end punch. Because the loop will go inside the key holder, it is important that you know the size you want it to be. For my key holder, I cut the strap 21 cm below the braid.

STEP 12 Make holes in the leather for the button studs. Begin by threading on the clasp (image b) and folding the key holder with the clasp placed exactly where you want it. Mark with an awl where you want the button studs to be on the front side (the short end below the braid). I placed them evenly spaced between the braid and the end of the strap. Make the holes using a keyhole-shaped punch on the marks you made with the awl (image c). An alternative is to use a revolving punch and a hobby knife. Fold the strap again and mark with an awl where the corresponding holes for the button studs should be placed (image d). Note! You should only make holes in the part of the strap that is folded 7 cm around the fastener. Make a round hole that fits the diameter of the button stud's post. Next, press the bottom of the button stud through the hole, insert the top of the button on the post and then carefully hit it with a rawhide mallet (image e).

STEP 13 Sew the strap together above, between and under the button studs: Use a pricking iron to make holes where the seams will be, and sew according to the instructions on page 35 (image f).

a.

b.

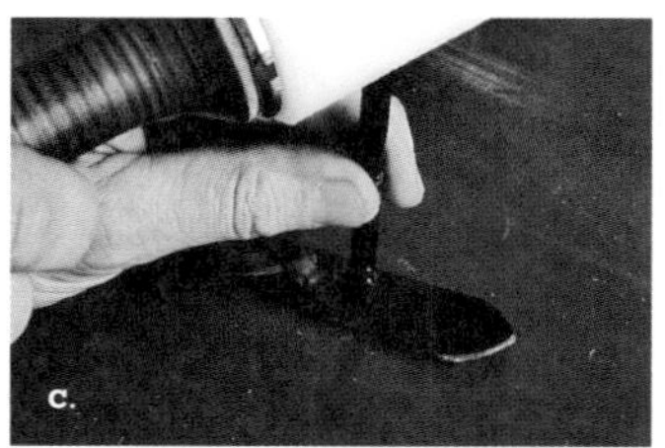
c.

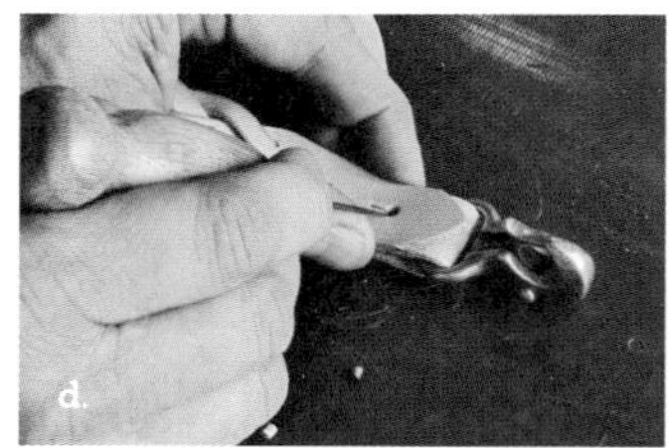
d.

e.

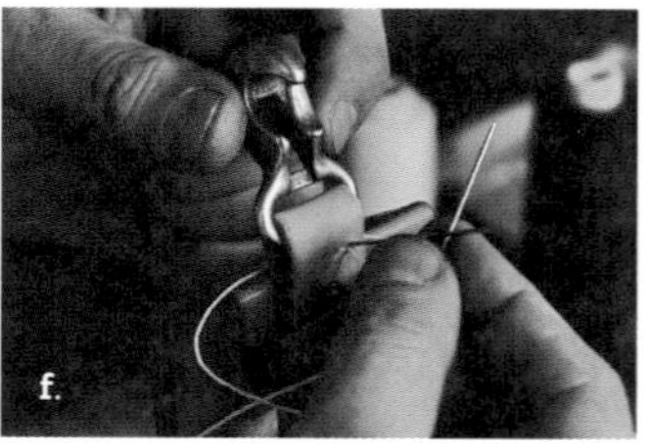
f.

LEATHER BOWL

WITH FOLDED CORNERS AND BRASS FASTENERS

MATERIALS

- 2 square leather pieces, 21 × 21 cm (makes a bowl that is 11 × 11 cm when it is folded together)
- 1.5–2 mm thick cardboard
- white paper and glue for the pattern
- 4 brass fasteners
- 8 brass eyelets and tool for setting them

TOOLS

- end punch for round corners or hobby knife
- slab for punching/striking
- pricking iron
- contact adhesive and brush
- ruler
- needle and thread for saddle stitching
- saddler's scratch or compass
- roller
- revolving punch
- rotary cutter
- rawhide mallet
- stitching pony
- cutting mat
- awl

STEP 1 Begin by drawing a square pattern on paper, preferably according to the specified dimensions. If you choose your own measurements, make the pattern an extra cm or two bigger than you think you'll need (the 1 cm margin is cut off after gluing). Cut out the pattern, glue it onto cardboard, and cut it out from the cardboard when the glue is dry. Using the pattern, cut out two pieces of leather.

STEP 2 Apply the adhesive on the flesh side of the leather pieces according to the instructions on page 28. When the glue has dried but is still tacky, press the two sides together. Be sure to put them edge to edge. Use a roller and press them together.

STEP 3 Cut the extra margin from the edges with the rotary knife; make sure the bowl is square. The grid on the cutting mat as well as your pattern are helpful guides for cutting 90-degree angles.

STEP 4 Round off all four corners with an end punch designed for corners or a hobby knife.

STEP 5 Mark where the holes for the fasteners should be on the leather using an awl. Adjust the size of the holes according to the size of the eyelet or fastener you have selected. Make holes in the leather with a revolving punch.

STEP 6 Mark where you will make your stitches with a scratch or compass along the edges of the leather. Then make holes with the pricking iron – use a smaller pricking iron with two teeth around the corners. Next, sew along the edges according to the instructions on page 35.

STEP 7 Set in the eyelets and fasteners.

COIN PURSE

WITH OPEN COMPARTMENT AND SNAP

MATERIALS

- 2 leather pieces for the inner and outer piece, 17 × 6.5 cm, 1.5 mm thick
- 1 snap and tool for setting it
- cardboard, white paper and glue for the patterns

TOOLS

- pricking iron
- coarse sandpaper
- hobby knife or Stanley knife blade
- slab for punching/striking
- burnisher or canvas cloth
- contact adhesive and brush
- ruler
- nail file
- needle and thread for saddle stitching
- saddler's scratch or compass
- burnishing fluid
- revolving punch
- rotary cutter
- raw gum eraser
- rawhide mallet or hammer
- cutting mat
- awl
- U-shaped end punch, about 40 mm wide

STEP 1 Begin by drawing a pattern on paper: It should be 17 cm tall and 6.5 cm wide. You can decide for yourself how the purse will look on the ends; I have used an English-point punch on the ends.

STEP 2 Cut out the pattern, glue it onto cardboard, allow the glue to dry then cut out the cardboard. Use the Stanley knife blade to cut the rounded corners; see page 24. The hole in the pattern is made with the U-shaped end punch. Place the hole so that you have room for both the snap and seam.

STEP 3 Use a sharp awl to make marks on the leather around your pattern and cut two identical leather pieces for the inner and outer pieces with a rotary cutter and ruler. Use the Stanley blade to cut the purse's rounded ends.

STEP 4 Place the snap on the inner part of the purse and mark with an awl on the leather where it will sit. Make two holes for the snap on the flesh side of the inner piece with a revolving punch and fasten it.

STEP 5 Make the hole in the inner piece with the end punch.

STEP 6 Use a nail file around the inner and outer pieces 5 mm in from the edge; file only on the leather's flesh side. Glue the leather pieces together according to the instructions on page 28. Be sure to put the pieces edge to edge.

STEP 7 Clean off any glue residue off the edges with a piece of eraser and file the edges evenly with a nail file. Then burnish the edges according to the instructions on page 39.

STEP 8 Mark where you are going to stitch with a scratch or compass about 3 mm from the edge of the purse. Make holes with the pricking iron along the marks and sew according to the instructions on page 35.

SEIKO
TANNER
GOODS

WALLET CHAIN

WITH ROUND BRAID AND BEADS

MATERIALS

2 leather straps, 150 cm × 6 mm, 1.5–2 mm thick
1 leather cord to tie the braid at the top = 50 cm × 6 mm, 1.5–2 mm thick
1 leather cord to thread beads on = 40 cm long with a thickness and width tailored to your beads
2 clasps with an opening at approximately 1.5 cm so the leather can be threaded through the beads for decoration

TOOLS

bag clip or other clip to hold together the braid when you need to take a break
strap cutter or ruler and rotary cutter
cutting mat
waxed synthetic thread
blunt awl or fid

STEP 1 Make a four-stranded round braid as instructed on page 50. Secure the braid when it is 35 cm long by tying it together with a waxed synthetic thread. Note! The braid should begin around the clasp that you plan to attach to the wallet.

STEP 2 Attach the second clasp to the loose end of the braid by making an end knot in the braid according to the instructions on page 54, but thread the strands through the clasp's ring when making the knot. Tighten the knot.

STEP 3 With the help of a fid, separate the strands of the braid a bit below the clasp and pull two of the strands through the braid so that they end up on the opposite side of each other (image a).

STEP 4 If you want to decorate your wallet chain with beads, thread the 40 cm long cord through the braid using the fid tool exactly as you did in step 3. Distribute the strands evenly around the braid.

STEP 5 Tie up the braid at the top. Take the 50 cm long cord and lay it along the length of the braid so that half of the strap is even with the fringes hanging down. Take the upper half of the cord and fold it at the top at the clasp so that you get a 5 cm wide loop (image b).

STEP 6 Start wrapping the upper half of the cord around the braid and its fringes; wrap from below and up to the clasp, not from the clasp down. Be careful that the fringes are evenly spaced around the braid as you wrap (image c).

STEP 7 When you get to the clasp, wrap the cord around the loop you made, but let a small part of the loop stick up from below the wrapped cord (image d). Once you have wound all the way up to the clasp, make an opening with the fid tool somewhere under the end knot next to the loop and pull the cord first through the loop and then through the opening you made with the fid under the end knot (image e). Now you can tighten the loop by pulling the lower end of the cord that is sticking up from under the wrapped cord (image f). Pull tight and cut off the rest of the cord you were wrapping with.

STEP 8 Finish off the braid by threading and tying the beads and then cutting the fringes to the desired length.

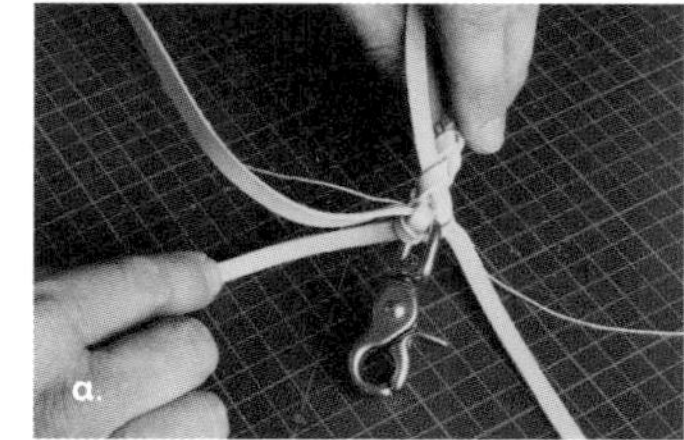

a.

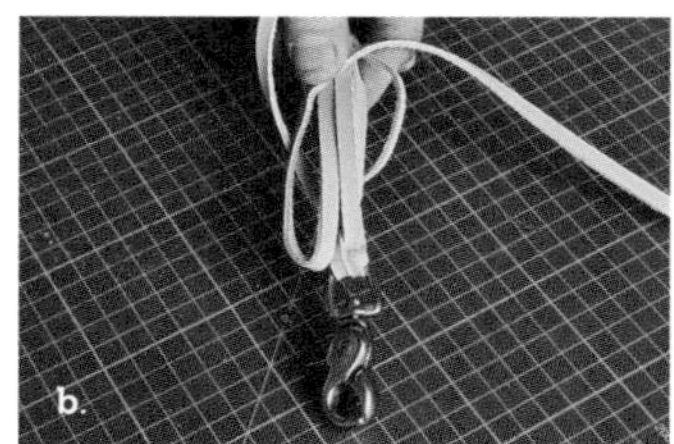

b.

c.

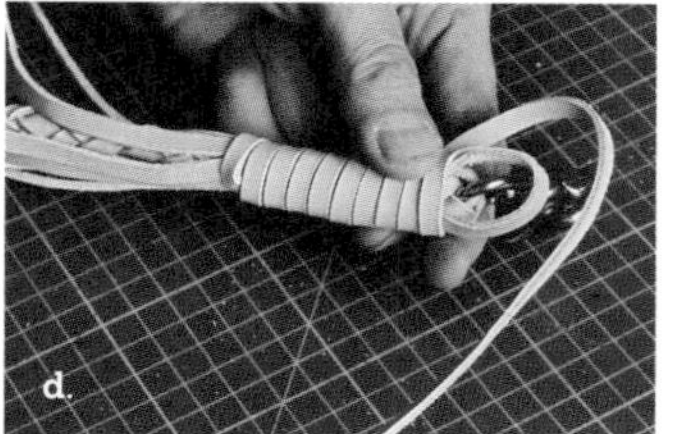

d.

e.

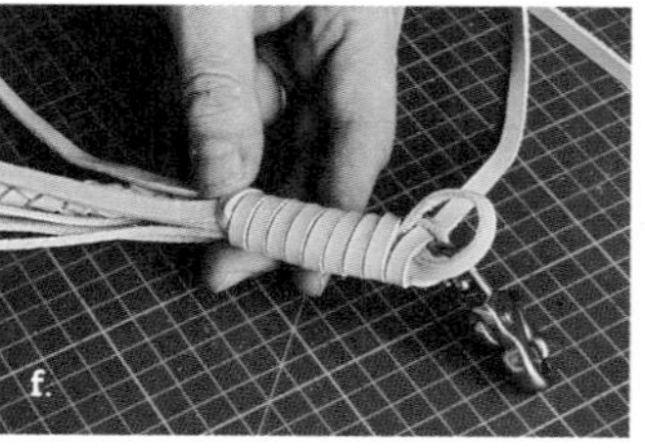

f.

POUCH

WITH ROUND-BRAIDED DRAWSTRING

MATERIALS

- 2 soft leather pieces for the front and back pieces, 15 × 12 cm, 1.5 mm thick
- 2 soft leather pieces for reinforcing, 5 × 10 cm, 1.5 mm thick.
- 4 leather straps for round braid with four strands, 60 cm × 3 mm, 1 mm thick
- 2 leather cords for drawstring, 10 × 1 cm, 1.5 mm thick.
- 1 fishhook clasp
- cardboard, white paper and glue for patterns

TOOLS

- pricking iron
- coarse sandpaper
- Stanley knife blade
- slab for punching/striking
- contact adhesive and brush
- ruler
- needle and thread for saddle stitching
- saddler's scratch or compass
- fid or sewing awl
- revolving punch
- rotary cutter
- stitching pony
- cutting mat
- awl
- rawhide mallet

STEP 1 Begin by drawing a pattern on paper: It should be 15 × 12 cm and round at one of the short ends. On the other short end, about 25 mm from the edge, place four 5 mm holes with 20 mm spacing in between (image a). Cut out the pattern, glue it onto cardboard, and cut the pattern out of the cardboard when the adhesive has dried.

STEP 2 Use a sharp awl to trace your pattern onto the leather, and cut two identical leather pieces for the front and back with a rotary blade and ruler. Use the Stanley knife blade to cut the round end, see page 25 (image b).

STEP 3 Place the pattern back down on the leather and make marks for the holes using the awl. Punch out the holes with a revolving punch.

STEP 4 Cut out two rectangular leather pieces to reinforce the upper part of the bag where the braid will be threaded through. The reinforcement pieces should be placed on the top of the pouch about 4 cm below the edge, with 1 cm folding over on the outside of the pouch. Mark with an awl 1 cm below the edge of the pouch's hair side and sand this surface with a piece of coarse sandpaper in preparation for gluing (image c). Mark with a pencil 4 cm below the edge of the pouch's flesh side to know where to apply the glue. Apply the glue and assemble the leather pieces according to the instructions on page 28. Glue and fold over 1 cm of the reinforcement so that it is on the outside of the pouch.

STEP 5 Mark where you are going to stitch with a scratch or compass along the reinforcement that is folded over the front and back pieces. Also mark a line 1 cm below the holes. Make stitching holes with the pricking iron, but not all the way out to the edge. Sew the reinforcement according to the instructions on page 35 (image d).

STEP 6 Mark with a scratch or compass about 3–4 mm from the edge along the long sides of the front and back pieces. Do this only on the hair side. Sand the surface only from the edge to the marks you just made 3–4 mm in with sandpaper. Apply glue to the sanded surface and join the front and back pieces (image e).

STEP 7 Use the scratch or compass again to make marks for stitching, this time about 5 mm from the edge around the entire pouch. Make stitching holes with the pricking iron and sew around the edges. Turn the pouch inside out.

STEP 8 Make a four-stranded round braid that's 30 cm long according to the instructions on page 50, and secure it with a Turk's head knot at one end. Tie a waxed synthetic thread around the other end.

STEP 9 Make two drawstrings of the 10 × 1 cm leather cords. Fold in the strap at both ends and sew a seam from edge to edge on the folded strap (image f). From the side, it should look like an eight. Attach the clasp to one of the drawstrings before sewing it together. The size of the loops in the drawstrings should be fitted to the braid. The braid should pass tightly through the drawstring.

STEP 10 Pull the loose end of the braid through the drawstring and then on through the four holes on the one side of the pouch. Then continue to thread the braid through the drawstring with the clasp and then through the four holes on the other side of the pouch and out through the first drawstring. Finish with a Turk's head knot at the end of the braid.

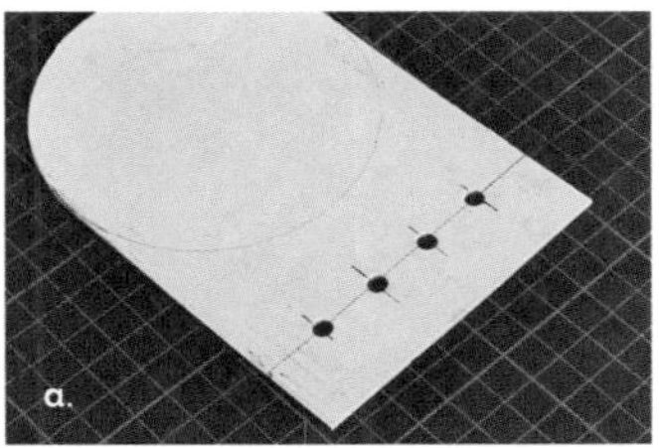
a.

b.

c.

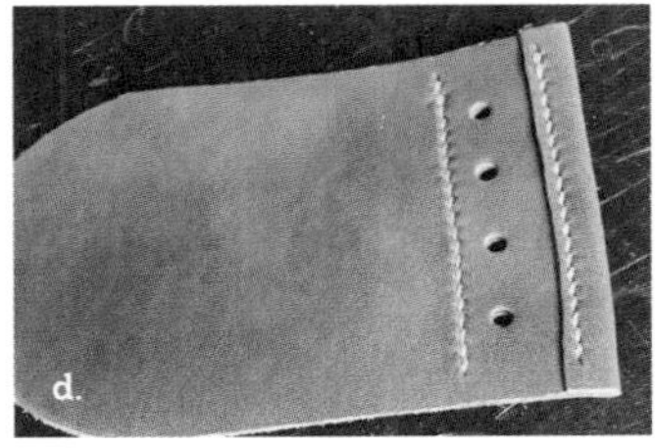
d.

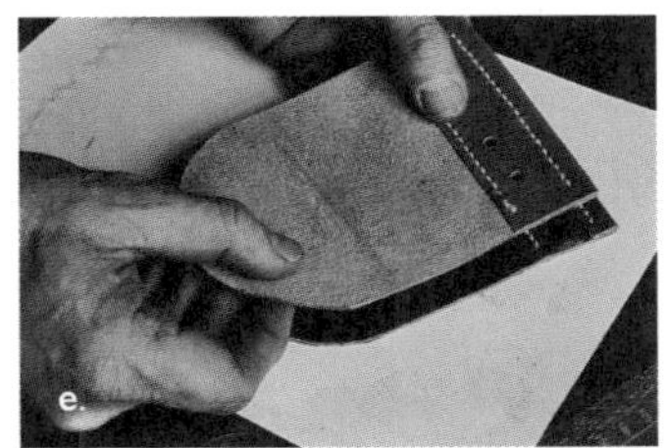
e.

f.

KEYCHAIN

WITH TURK'S HEAD OR GAUCHO KNOT

MATERIALS FOR TURK'S HEAD KNOT

- 2 leather straps, 80 cm × 6 mm, 1.5–2 mm thick
- 1 leather cord to thread beads on, 45 cm long with a thickness and width adapted to the beads
- 1 key ring and/or clasp with an opening of approx 1.5 cm so the leather can be threaded through
- beads for decoration

MATERIALS FOR A GAUCHO KNOT

- 2 leather cords, 100 cm × 6 mm, 1.5–2 mm
- 1 key ring and/or clasp with an opening of about 1.5 cm so the leather can be threaded through
- beads for decoration

TOOLS

- fid or lacing awl
- bag clip or clip to hold together the braid when you need to take a break
- strap cutter or ruler and rotary cutter
- cutting mat
- waxed synthetic thread

WITH A TURK'S HEAD KNOT:

STEP 1 Make a four-stranded round braid around a clasp according to the instructions on page 50. When you begin the braid, include the extra cord so you can thread the beads on it and braid around it. Secure the braid when it is 10 cm long by tying it together with a waxed synthetic thread.

STEP 2 Make an end knot according to the instructions on page 54, but do not tighten the knot. Continue by making a Turk's head knot as described on page 53.

STEP 3 Finish the braid by threading and tying beads and cutting the fringes to desired length.

WITH A GAUCHO KNOT:

STEP 1 Make a four-stranded round braid around a clasp according to the instructions on page 50. Secure the braid when it is 12 cm long by tying it with a waxed synthetic thread.

STEP 2 Make an end knot according to the instructions on page 54, tighten it, and be sure to make it even as it will be visible on the top of the gaucho knot. Continue making a gaucho knot as shown on page 55.

STEP 3 Finish the braid by cutting off the strands that stick out from the bottom of the knot.

BRAIDED KEY RING

WITH FISHHOOK CLASP

MATERIALS

3 leather straps, 80 cm × 4 mm, 1.5–2 mm thick
1 leather cord to thread beads on, 45 cm with a thickness and width adapted to your beads
1 key ring and/or clasp with an opening of approximately 1.5 cm so the leather can be threaded through
beads for decoration

TOOLS

fid or lacing awl
bag clip or other clip to hold together the braid when you need to take a break
strap cutter or ruler and rotary cutter
cutting mat
waxed synthetic thread

STEP 1 Make a six-stranded round braid around a clasp according to the instructions on page 52. When you begin the braid, include the extra cord so you can thread the beads on it and braid around it. Secure the braid when it is 12 cm long by tying it together with a waxed synthetic thread.

STEP 2 Make an end knot according to the instructions on page 54, but do not tighten the knot. Continue by making a Turk's head knot as shown on page 53.

STEP 3 Finish the braid by threading the beads onto the strands and cutting the fringes to the desired length.

BRAIDED WALLET CHAIN

WITH BEADS AND LONG FRINGES

⤜→ MATERIALS

- 3 leather straps, 150 cm × 4 mm, 1.5–2 mm thick
- 1 leather cord to tie the braid at the top = 50 cm × 6 mm, 1.5–2 mm thick
- 1 leather cord to thread beads on, 40 cm long with a thickness and width tailored to your beads
- 2 clasps with an opening at approximately 1.5 cm so the leather can be threaded through the beads for decoration

⤜→ TOOLS

- ruler
- fid or sewing awl
- bag clip or clip to hold the braid together when you need to take a break
- strap cutter or ruler and rotary cutter
- cutting mat
- waxed synthetic thread

STEP 1 Make a six-stranded round braid around a clasp according to the instructions on page 52. Secure the braid when it is 35 cm long by tying it together with a waxed synthetic thread.

STEP 2 Separate the braid's six strands into three and three. Braid two three-stranded braids that are 2–3 cm long, and put the clip around the first braid to hold it in place while doing the second (image a). Once you have braided both, thread the other three-strand braid through the ring of your other clasp and pull down on the clasp's end (image b).

STEP 3 Scissor the first braid's three strands with the three strands from the other braid (image c). Use the clip to hold the strands in place and braid two three-strand braids that are 4 cm long (image d).

STEP 4 Using a fid or lacing tool, thread one strand from each braid through the round braid so that the braids end up facing each other (images e and f).

STEP 5 If you want to decorate your braid with beads, thread the 40 cm long cord through the braid exactly as you did with the other strands in step 4. Arrange the strands/fringes evenly around the braid.

STEP 6 Tie the braid at the top. Take the 50 cm long cord and lay it along the length of the braid so that one half of the cord is even with the braid's fringes. Take the upper half of the cord and fold it at the top at the clasp so that you get a 5 cm wide loop (image b on page 82).

STEP 7 Then start wrapping the upper half of the cord around the braid and its fringes; wrap from below and up to the clasp, not from the clasp down. Be careful that the fringes are evenly spaced around the braid as you wrap. When approaching the clasp, wrap the cord around the loop you made, but let a small part of the loop stick up from below the wrapped cord (image d on page 82). Once wound all the way up to the clasp, pull the cord through the loop. Using a fid or lacing tool, thread the cord between the three-strand braid and the six-strand braid. Now, you can tighten the loop by pulling the lower end of the cord that is sticking up from under the wrapped cord. Pull tight and cut off the rest of the cord you were wrapping with.

STEP 8 Finish off the braid by threading the beads onto the strands and tying the ends, then cutting the fringes to the desired length.

a.

b.

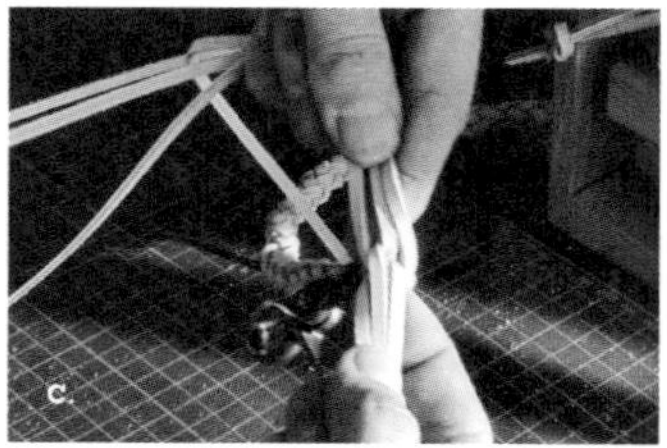
c.

d.

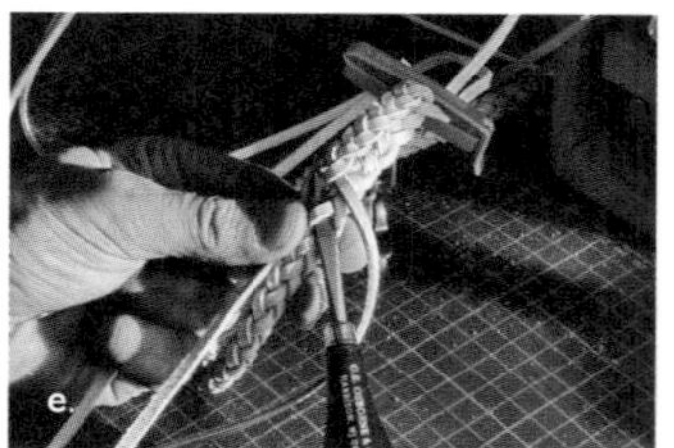
e.

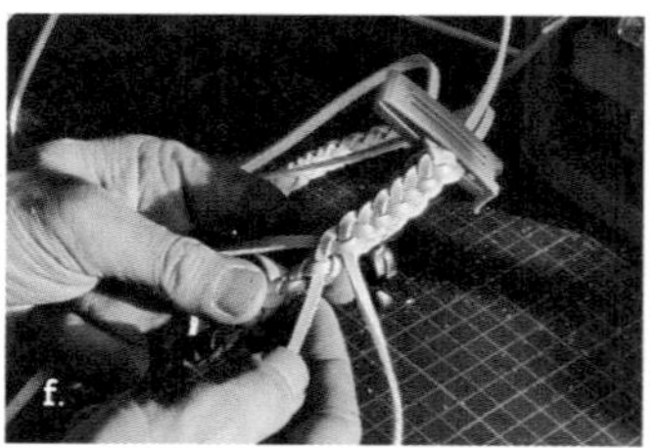
f.

ENVELOPE-STYLE CELL PHONE CASE

WITH SEWN-IN SNAP

STEP 1 Begin by cutting out a mold with the same dimensions as your cell phone from a plastic cutting board. Cheap cutting boards are available in most department stores.

STEP 2 Draw a pattern for the front and back parts of the case on paper (image a). Use the same measurements as your cell phone, but add an extra margin to the width and length as indicated. To test the patterns and know where to put the snap, you can make them out of thinner paper and staple them together at the edges.

STEP 3 Use a sharp awl to trace your patterns onto the leather, then cut two identical leather pieces for the front and two for the back with a rotary cutter and ruler. Cut out the round corners of the leather with a hobby knife or an end punch designed for round corners.

STEP 4 Use your patterns and a sharp awl to mark the holes on the leather where the snap should sit. Because the snap will be hidden, mark only one of the front and one of the back leather pieces. Don't make the holes yet.

STEP 5 Cut out the round piece of leather that you will sew onto the top of the snap. Mark where you are going to sew the seam using a compass set to 2 mm around the edge of the round leather piece. Burnish the edge as instructed on page 39.

STEP 6 Now sew a decorative stitch around the half of the snap button that is also on the front piece. Set the compass to a 21 mm diameter, place it in the center of the mark where you will later make a hole for the snap and make a circle (image b).

STEP 7 Take the back piece that you did not mark in step 4. With the compass set to 21 mm, mark a circle around where the round leather piece will be glued and sewn, that is, in the same

»——→ MATERIALS

- 2 leather pieces for the front part, 2–2.5 cm wider and 1–1.25 cm longer than the cell phone's dimensions
- 2 leather pieces for the back piece, same width and twice as long as the front piece
- 1 round leather piece, 25 mm in diameter, 1 mm thick
- 1 snap and tool for setting it
- cardboard, white paper and glue for patterns
- 1 mold in wood or plastic

»——→ TOOLS

- pricking iron
- hobby knife or end punch for round corners
- slab for punching / striking
- burnisher or canvas cloth
- contact adhesive and brush
- ruler or slide rule
- nail file or sandpaper
- needle and thread for saddle stitching
- saddler's scratch or compass
- burnishing fluid
- cutting mat
- rotary knife
- rawhide mallet
- gum eraser
- stitching pony
- awl

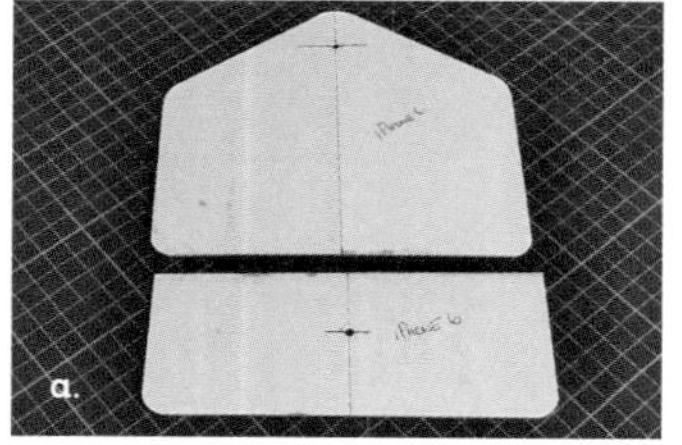
a.

b.

c.

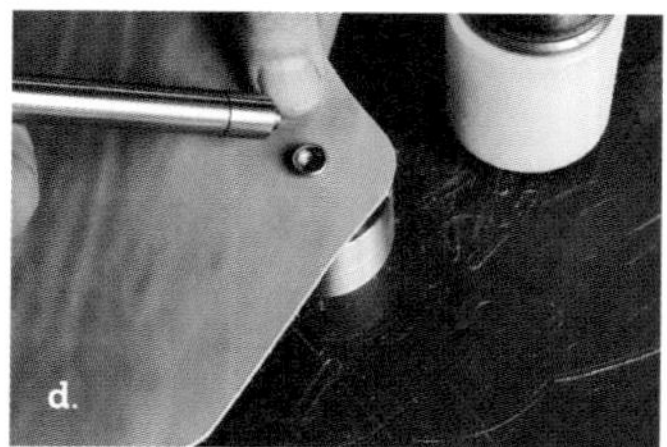
d.

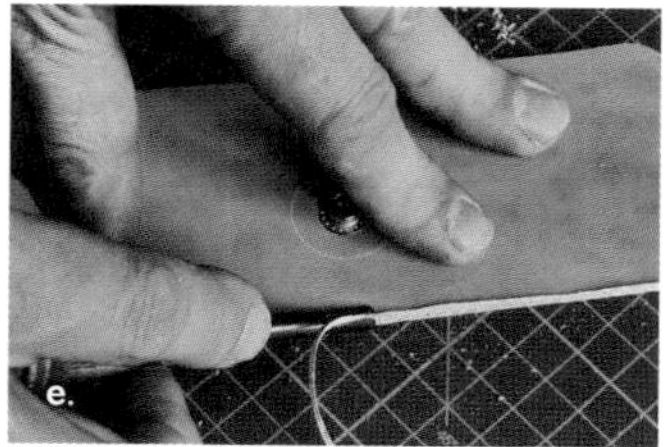
e.

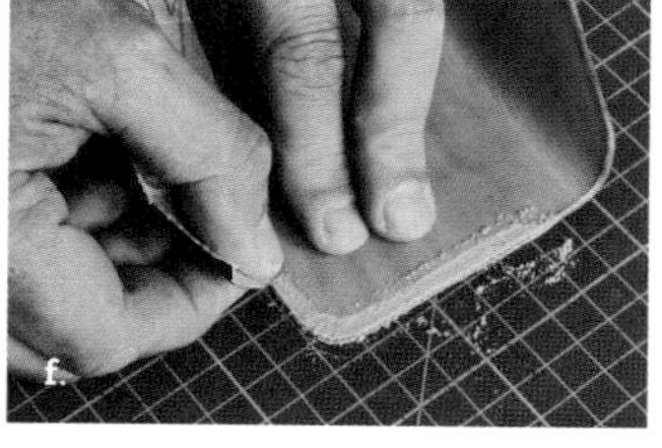
f.

place that the snap will be (image c). Then sand the area inside the circle with a coarse sandpaper and glue the round leather piece to the sanded surface according to the instructions on page 28.

STEP 8 Make a hole for the snap with a revolver punch in the leather pieces that you marked in step 4. Set the snaps in the holes (image d).

STEP 9 Glue together the two parts of the front and back pieces, flesh side against flesh side. You will now have two pieces, a front piece and a back piece, with the hair side on both sides. Be sure to put them edge to edge. File off glue residue from the edges with a nail file. Trim the top edges of the front and back pieces (image e) and burnish the upper edge of the front piece.

STEP 10 Before gluing together the front and back pieces, sew a decorative seam along the top edge of the front, around the snap on the front piece and around the round leather piece on the back piece's outside. Use a compass to mark along the top edge of the front piece, then make stitching holes with a pricking iron around the round leather piece, snap and the front edge of the front piece. The seam on the top edge of the front piece should end about 5 mm from the edge. Sew according to the instructions on page 35.

STEP 11 Place the front piece on top of the back piece and mark with an awl on the back piece how much you should file for gluing. File the area inside the marking on the back piece (image f) and on the corresponding surface of the front piece. Apply glue and attach the two parts.

STEP 12 Mark where you will do the stitching with a compass around the front piece's edges. Make stitching holes with the pricking iron. To make sure that the seam stitches will go in the same direction on the front piece and the outside of the back piece, the stitching must be done in two stages: first through the front piece and then through the upper part of the back piece from the outside. Sew the edge of the front piece first and secure the thread, then sew the upper edge of the back piece.

STEP 13 Clean the edge of the case of any glue residue with a piece of eraser and file the edges evenly with a hard nail file. Burnish the edges.

ROUND BRAIDED BRACELET

WITH A ROUND KNOT

MATERIALS

SIX STRANDS

3 kangaroo leather straps, 100 cm × 3 mm, 1 mm thick
1 round leather cord for core in the braid, 3 mm thick, length to fit wrist (close-fitting)

EIGHT STRANDS

4 kangaroo leather straps, 100 cm × 3 mm, 1 mm thick
1 round leather cord for core in the braid, 3 mm thick, length to fit wrist (close-fitting)

TOOLS

fid or lacing awl
bag clip or clip to hold the braid together when you need to take a break
strap cutter or ruler and rotary cutter
cutting mat
waxed synthetic thread

STEP 1 Begin by folding the three or four straps in the middle and putting a clip a few centimeters from the center. Make sure the hair side of all the straps is facing upward.

STEP 2 Thread the longer straps into your support and pull them through until the clip fastens behind the support (image a). You must be able to remove the support when braiding is complete.

STEP 3 Make a flat braid with three strands or a round braid with four strands as instructed on page 50 (image b). This part of the braid will form the loop in the bracelet. With the 3 mm wide kangaroo leather straps, I braided about 7 turns. The round knot at the other end of the bracelet will be about 1 cm in diameter. The loop should fit snugly around the knot.

STEP 4 Make a transition from a three-stranded flat braid to a six-stranded round braid, or from a four-stranded round braid to an eight-stranded one according to the instructions on page 52.

STEP 5 After crossing the strands according to the instructions, insert the round cord you intend to use as the core of the loop (image c). You will correct the cord's position after braiding a few turns. Braid four turns and then gently pull the strands around the core. Now you can put the core in place so that it is at the beginning of the bracelet (image d). Note! With a round braid of eight strands, it is possible to vary the braid. You can make an eight-stranded round braid by braiding a strand under, a strand over, a strand under, a strand over. If you want to braid a herringbone pattern, braid two strands under and two strands over (image e). However, closest to the loop, you should still braid two turns with the regular pattern.

STEP 6 Continue braiding until you reach the other end of the core, that is, the full length of the bracelet.

STEP 7 Tie the braid together with a waxed synthetic thread so that it does not unravel. Secure the braid by making a round knot as instructed on page 55 (image f). The round knot does not require a core. As you make the knot, the leather may feel stiff at first, but it should stretch out.

a.

b.

c.

d.

e.

f.

KNIFE SHEATH

FOR A 13 CM × 2 CM × 6 MM HIGONAKAMI KNIFE

MATERIALS

1 leather piece for the front, 12 × 4.8 cm, 2 mm thick
1 leather piece for the back, 23 × 4.8 cm, 2 mm thick
1 leather piece for the belt loop = 10 × 2.5 cm, 2 mm thick
1 leather piece for the button, 35 mm in diameter, 4 mm thick
1 leather piece for drawstring casing, 35 mm in diameter, 1 mm thick
4 leather cords, 50 cm × 3 mm, 1 mm thick

TOOLS

oblong punch, approx. 12 mm
pricking iron
slab for punching/striking
burnisher or canvas cloth
edge beveler
lacing needle
nail file or sandpaper
needle and thread for saddle stitching
saddler's scratch or compass
polishing fluid
strap cutter
revolving punch
gum eraser
rotary cutter
stitching pony
awl
U-shaped end punch

STEP 1 Start by using a strap cutter to cut out a strap that is 35 cm long × 4.8 cm wide. Use the rotary cutter to cut the strap into a 12 cm long piece for the front of the sheath and a 23 cm long piece for the back.

STEP 2 Cut out the button and drawstring. Since it is easier to cut thinner leather, the button can also be made by gluing together two pieces that are 2 mm thick.

STEP 3 Place the drawstring casing on the front piece and carefully mark around it with an awl (image a). When the front and back pieces are glued together, you will cut off the end of the sheath with an end punch, so do not place the drawstring casing too close to the lower edge of the front piece.

STEP 4 Use the compass to mark where to make the stitches around the edge of the button and drawstring casing (image b). Burnish the edge of the button and drawstring casing according to the instructions on page 39.

STEP 5 Use an awl to mark where to put the holes for the button and drawstring casing (image c). To make the holes symmetrical, you can make cardboard patterns and use them for marking where the holes will be. Then, make two holes in the button with an oblong punch and four holes in the drawstring casing with the revolving punch.

STEP 6 Use a nail file to file the surface inside the mark you made for the drawstring casing in step 3. The drawstring casing should not be glued completely, so it is sufficient to file only 5 mm in from the marking.

STEP 7 Apply glue around the outer edge of the drawstring casing and to the filed surface of the front piece. When the glue is still a bit tacky, put the leather pieces together and press them with a roller.

a.

b.

c.

d.

e.

f.

STEP 8 Make stitching holes with the pricking iron on the marks you made around the drawstring casing and button. Sew the drawstring casing to the front piece and sew a decorative stitch around the button as instructed for saddle stitching on page 35.

STEP 9 Cut a strap for the belt loop with the strap cutter. Burnish the edges and then sew the belt loop to the back of the knife sheath (image d).

STEP 10 Glue the front and back pieces together as instructed on page 28. Be sure to put the leather pieces edge to edge. Press the glued pieces with a roller.

STEP 11 Cut off the ends of the sheath with the U-shaped end punch (image e). Clean off any glue residue and file the edges evenly with a hard nail file.

STEP 12 Mark where you will stitch with the compass along the edges of the sheath. Trim the edges around the sheath (image f). File the edges with a nail file.

STEP 13 Make stitching holes with the pricking iron along the markings you made in step 12. When the sheath is closed, the front and back of the cover will be visible (see project image). To ensure that the seam stitches of both parts go in the same direction, they must be made in two stages: first, through the front piece and then through the upper part of the back piece from the outside of the back.

STEP 14 Burnish the edges around the entire sheath. Sew the sheath in two stages: Sew around the edge of the front piece and secure the thread, then, sew around the edge of the upper part of the back piece.

STEP 15 Place the button on the top of the back piece and use it as a pattern to mark where to put the two holes with the oblong punch in the back piece. Cut a strap as wide as the holes in the button and pull it through the button and the back piece. Braid the strap as a hole braid as instructed on page 46 to hold the button in place.

STEP 16 Make a 25 cm long round braid with four strands, as instructed on page 50, and secure it with a Turk's head knot at one end. With a lacing needle, thread the four strands through the holes in the drawstring casing. When the braid has been pulled through, make a Turk's head knot at the other end of the braid.

WALLET

WITH DECORATIVE STUDS AND BRAIDED CHAIN

MATERIALS

- 1 leather piece for the wallet's exterior, 18 × 20 cm, 1.5 mm thick
- 2 leather pieces for the wallet's money pocket, 8 × 20 cm, 1.5 mm thick
- 2 leather pieces for the wallet's credit card pocket, 8 × 20 cm, 1.5 cm thick
- 2 snaps and setting tool
- brass eyelets
- decorative studs
- cardboard, white paper and glue for patterns

TOOLS

- pricking iron
- hobby knife
- end punch for round corners
- slab for punching/striking
- burnisher or canvas cloth
- edge beveler
- contact adhesive and brush
- ruler
- nail file or sandpaper
- needle and thread for saddle stitching
- saddler's scratch or compass
- burnishing fluid
- revolving punch
- rotary cutter
- rawhide mallet
- cutting mat
- Stanley knife blade
- awl

STEP 1 Start by making patterns according to the specified dimensions: one for the wallet's exterior, one for the wallet's banknote pocket, and one for the wallet's credit card pocket. All should have the same width, but the shape of the upper edge of the compartments can be varied. I have used a curved pattern to make it rounded, but you can make the pockets according to your own design. Mark where to put the holes for the snaps in the corners at the bottom of the credit card pattern, about 1.5 cm from the edge. Draw your patterns on paper, cut and glue them onto cardboard and then cut them out again.

STEP 2 Mark with a sharp awl on the leather around your patterns and cut out the leather pieces with a rotary cutter and ruler.

STEP 3 Use the pattern and the awl again to mark all the round shapes. Cut out the rounded shapes with a hobby knife (image a).

STEP 4 Round off the outermost corners with an end punch for round corners or a Stanley knife blade – see page 24.

STEP 5 Trim the upper edge of all four inner pockets and then burnish the upper edge of all four inner pockets as instructed on page 39.

STEP 6 Use the pattern and the awl to mark the leather where the holes for the snaps should be on the credit card pocket. Make holes with the revolving punch and set the snaps (image b).

STEP 7 Prepare the edges of the money and credit card pockets for gluing, 5 mm from the edges, according to the instructions on page 28. Glue together the money and credit card pockets, and be sure to put them edge to edge.

STEP 8 To divide the credit card pocket into two parts, sew a seam in the middle. Mark the center of the pocket, 10 cm from the sides, with an awl. Make stitching holes with the pricking iron along the marking but not all the way to the lower edge of the leather, and then sew as instructed on page 35 (image c).

STEP 9 Punch with a stamp (see page 41), and attach any decorative studs to the outside of the wallet (image d).

STEP 10 Glue the two attached credit card and money pockets to the wallet's exterior, taking care to put the leather pieces edge to edge.

STEP 11 A square leather piece is fitted and glued into the gap between the pockets. This is where the brass eyelet for the wallet chain will be attached.

STEP 12 Clean the edges of any glue residue with a piece of eraser and file the edges evenly with a hard nail file.

STEP 13 Measure the thickness of the wallet and mark where to make the seam with a compass along the wallet's edges (image e). The distance of the stitch from the edge should be approximately the same as the wallet's thickness.

STEP 14 Make stitching holes with the pricking iron on the marking and sew around the wallet (image f).

STEP 15 Finish by burnishing the wallet's edges according to the instructions on page 39.

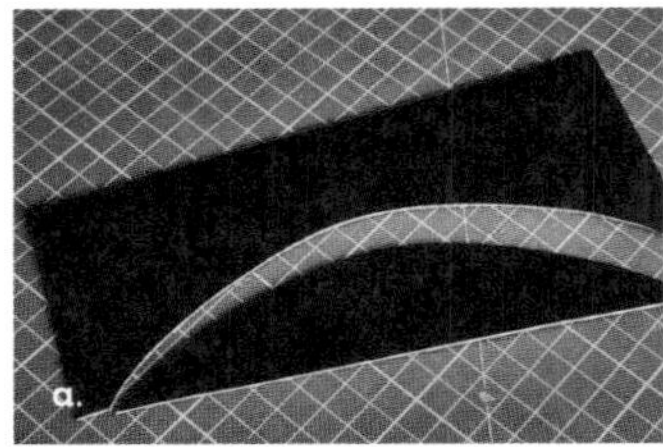
a.

b.

c.

d.

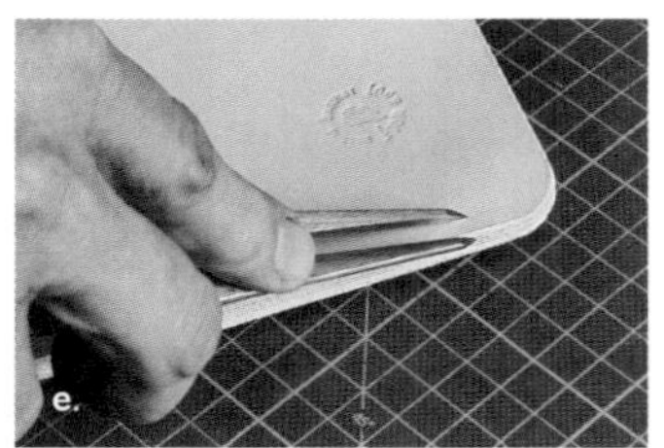
e.

f.

BELT

WITH BUCKLE AND BRASS LOOP

MATERIALS

- 1 leather strap for the belt, with a width adjusted to your buckle and end punch and a length you decide, but add 30 cm
- 1 optional leather strap for a loop, 10 cm × 15 mm, 2.5 mm thick
- 1 buckle
- cardboard for the pattern

TOOLS

- oblong punch, 25–30 mm depending on thickness of the buckle's loop
- English point end punch
- diamond-shaped awl
- pricking iron
- slab for punching/striking
- burnisher or canvas cloth
- edge beveler
- ruler
- measuring tape
- needle and thread for saddle stitch
- saddler's scratch or compass
- burnishing compound
- strap cutter
- rotary cutter
- revolving punch
- round punch
- rawhide mallet
- wood creaser or creasing iron
- stitching pony

STEP 1 The width of your belt is determined primarily by the buckle you select. You may also need to take into account the width of your end punch if you use it to cut the ends of the belt. The belt does not have to sit tight in the buckle; on the contrary, it is good with a little play. So, if your buckle is a bit wider than your end punch, go with the end punch's width instead. The alternative to an end punch is to use the blade of a Stanley knife together with a rawhide mallet to cut off the ends of the belt.

STEP 2 Make a pattern 30 cm long in cardboard with the same width as your belt. Use a slide rule to measure and mark a center line on the pattern. Mark along the center line where you will have five round holes with approximately 2.5 cm of spacing in between. Make holes in the pattern with a revolving punch or a round punch. On the center line, also make an oblong hole, the length is determined by the buckle but approximately 25–30 mm usually suffices (image a).

STEP 3 Set the strap cutter to the width of the pattern and the thickness of the leather, and cut out the belt. Cut one end of the belt with an English point end punch or Stanley knife blade.

STEP 4 Use a ruler or tape measure to measure and mark 20 cm from the belt's cut-off end; this is where the third hole of the five will be (image b). Take the pattern and mark all five holes with a pointed awl onto the leather. Then make the holes with the revolving punch or a round punch.

STEP 5 The length measured from the third round hole to the belt buckle determines the size of the belt. Use a tape measure and, based on the third of the five round holes, measure and mark where you will make the oblong hole where the belt buckle will sit. Then take the pattern and mark the oblong hole with a pointed awl on the leather. Then make the hole with an oblong punch. It is also possible to do this with a revolving

punch and a shortened Stanley knife blade; in this case, make two round holes with the revolving hole punch, and then punch out the leather between the holes with the Stanley blade and a rawhide mallet (image c).

STEP 6 Cut off the other end of the belt with a U-shaped end punch or Stanley knife blade approximately 10 cm from the oblong hole.

STEP 7 Trim the edges of the belt and burnish the edges as instructed on page 39. If you want to make a decorative line with a wooden creaser or creasing iron, do so now.

STEP 8 Mark where you will stitch with a compass along the edges of the 10 cm long end you left after the oblong hole. This end, which folds around the buckle, may need to be thinned depending on the belt's thickness. Use a skiving knife for this – see page 40.

STEP 9 Fold the 10 cm long end around the buckle. To make it easier to fold the leather, you can lightly moisten it where it will be folded. Once you have gotten the buckle in place, make the stitching holes with a pricking iron where you previously marked with the compass. Make the holes along one edge first and then sew 3–4 stitches as instructed on page 35 to keep the leather folded and in place. Now you can make the holes along the other edge and finish sewing (image d).

STEP 10 Some belts need a leather loop right next to the buckle to hold the end of the belt in place. To make a loop, use a thinner leather and cut a strap to the desired width. The strap should be long enough to reach around the strap plus a little extra. Trim the edges, decorate and burnish the strap. Wrap the strap around the belt where it is going to sit. To measure the exact length, tighten the belt in the loop (the belt should sit tight in the loop) and then cut the strap to the right length (image e). Sew on the loop while sewing on the buckle: Do exactly as in step 9, but thread the loop in when you make the stitching holes with the pricking iron along one edge so that the holes go through both the belt and the loop. Next, sew along the first edge. Continue to make the stitching holes along the other edge, again through both the loop and the belt, and then sew (image f). For the other edge, a diamond-shaped awl may be needed if it is difficult to reach it with the pricking iron.

»⟶ TOOLS, CONTINUED

slide rule
Stanley knife blade
skiving knife depending on the leather's thickness
cutting mat
awl
U-shaped end punch

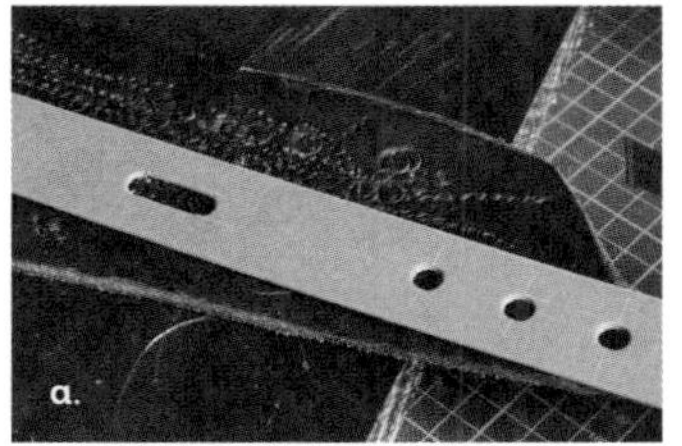
a.

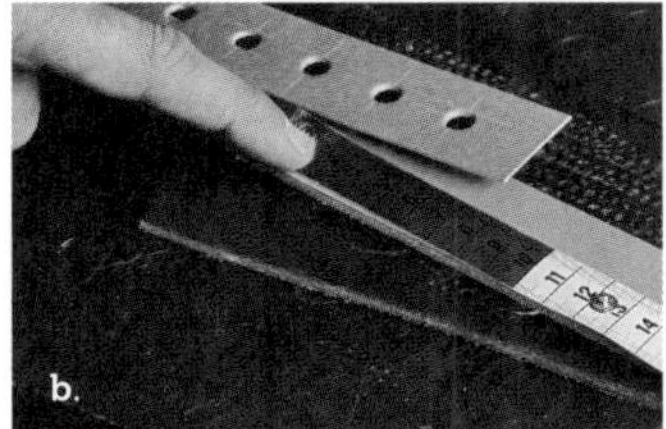
b.

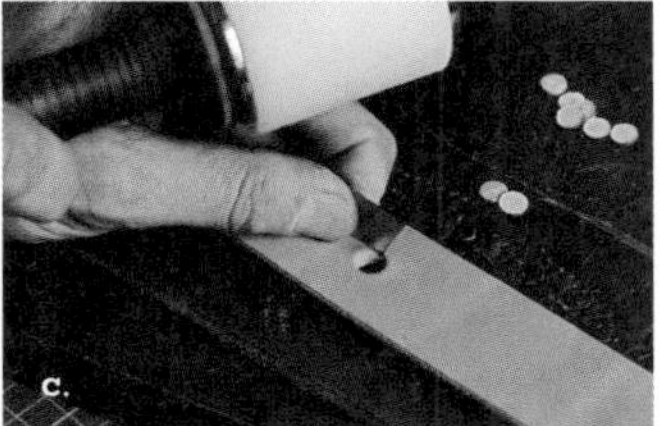
c.

d.

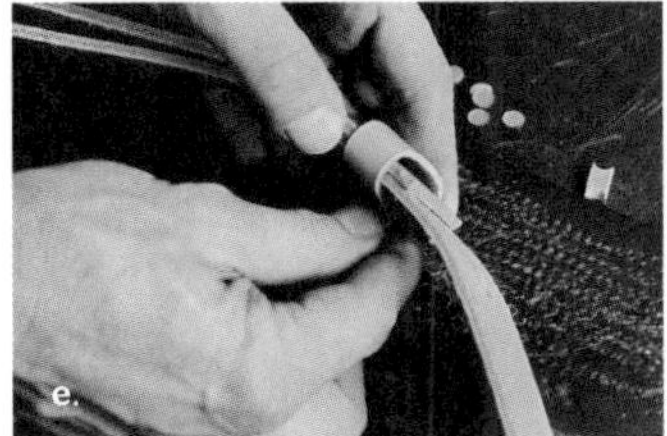
e.

f.

TIPS! To shape the loop and make it easier to thread it in, you can cut a plastic wedge from a cheap cutting board. The wedge should be the width and thickness of the belt. Sew on the loop so that it is nearly or too tight to thread in the belt end. Wet the loop and then insert the wedge. Once the leather has dried your loop will be perfectly shaped to sit tightly around the belt.

SEIKO

POCKET WATCH

WITH CLIP AND BRAIDED LEATHER CHAIN

MATERIALS

2 pieces of leather for the back, 65 mm in diameter (or customized to your watch), 1–1.5 mm thick
leather for watch band, 16.5 cm × 22 mm, 1–1.5 mm thick (or customized to your watch)
cardboard, white paper and glue for the patterns

TOOLS

oblong punch or revolving punch
hobby knife
slab for punching/striking
burnisher or canvas cloth
contact adhesive and brush
ruler
nail file
needle and thread for saddle stitching
saddler's scratch or compass
polishing fluid
cutting mat
strap cutter
eraser
rawhide mallet
stitching pony slide
rule awl
U-shaped end punch

STEP 1 Start by making a pattern for the back piece of the pocket watch. Measure the watch's diameter; the back piece should be about 2 cm larger in diameter than the watch. Also check how thick of a band your watch can have – usually a thickness of about 1.5 mm works for both the back piece and the band. Make a hole in the pattern that shows where the band is to be threaded through the back piece. You can see where the holes should sit by placing the watch in the middle of the pattern and tracing around it. Make a hole in the pattern with an oblong punch or with a revolving punch and a knife where the two pins for the watch strap are traced (image a). Make the holes a bit wider than your traced watch.

STEP 2 Mark with a sharp awl on the leather around your pattern and cut out the back piece with a sharp hobby knife. A Japanese circle compass leather cutter would be suitable for this – see page 24. You need two pieces: one for the front side and one for the back side of the back piece.

STEP 3 Make the holes for the watch band with an oblong punch in the leather piece that will be the front side of the back piece. If you do not have a punch with the exact size, you can use a smaller one and make multiple holes until you get one of the desired size. You can also use a revolving punch and a sharp knife. If you do that, make the holes with the revolving punch first and then fold the leather so that the two holes are on top of each other. Place a sharp knife at the edge of the hole, and make sure the cut is as wide as the hole. Now you can cut with the knife through both layers of leather. Do the same along the other outer edge of the hole. You do not need to make any holes in the back of the back piece.

STEP 4 Make a pattern for the watch band. Measure the width that fits your watch and the width of any buckle that will sit on the band. The watch in the picture has a band that is 22 mm wide and a clip that is 7 mm wide. Make a pattern with a width that will fit both the watch and the clip. The pattern should be a bit longer than you think is needed. The exact length is adjusted in the next step.

STEP 5 Set the strap cutter to the width of the pattern and the thickness of the leather. Cut out your band. Make two semi-circle cuts at one end of your pattern and use the pattern and a U-shaped punch to make the cuts in the leather band (image b). The clip will be sitting where the semi-circles are made. The band will be folded in two places and the folds are brought up through the holes in the back of the back piece to form two loops attached to the watch pins (image e). The ends of the band will be folded down and the semi-circles at one end will form a narrow loop that will fit your clip (image e). Use the back piece to mark on the band where the folds need to sit in order to go through the holes on the back piece. Try inserting the band into the back piece to find out exactly what length it should have, and cut the ends if necessary. The ends should be short enough to be folded under and glued in step 7. Once you know the length of the band, you can adjust the length of the pattern for next time.

STEP 6 Now, measure the combined thickness of the two back pieces – this measurement will be a guide to how close to the edge you should put your saddle stitch. Both pieces of leather together should be about 3 mm. Mark with a compass or slide rule 3 mm from the edge on the front of the back piece.

STEP 7 Fold the strap over in two places and thread the folds through the holes in the front side of the back piece. Adjust the size of the loops on the front side. The loops cannot be adjusted afterwards, so keep in mind that they should not be so big that the watch sits loosely or so small that the pins of the watch cannot pass through. Also, adjust the size of the loop that the clip will sit in. When you are happy with how the band is sitting, it's time to glue. Apply adhesive to the flesh side of the band and to its ends (image d). When the glue is dry, fold over the ends and press them with a roller so that they are fastened to the band's flesh side. Apply adhesive to the entire surface of the back piece, including the top of the folded end of the band. Also apply adhesive to the other part of the back piece (image c). When the glue has dried sufficiently, put the two parts of the back piece together. Be sure to place them edge to edge (image e)

a.

b.

c.

d.

e.

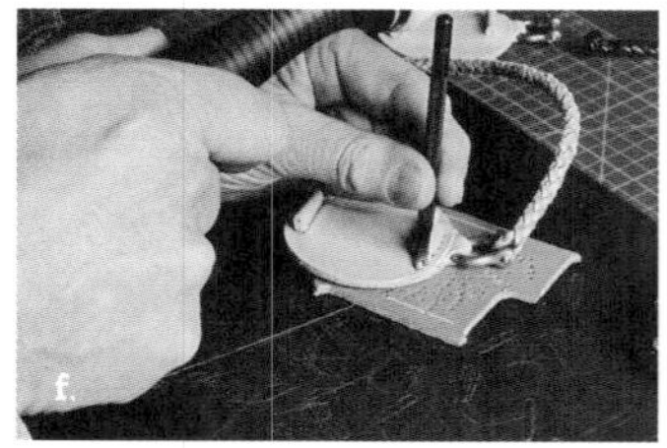
f.

"ATTACH A CHAIN TO A POCKET WATCH, OR WHY NOT MAKE YOUR OWN BRAIDED LEATHER CHAIN WITH A KNOT?"

STEP 8 Now it's time to make the stitching holes with a pricking iron (image f). It is easiest to use a pricking iron with two teeth with a distance between the teeth of about 3–4 mm.

STEP 9 Sew around the entire back piece as instructed on page 35. Start the seam on the lower part of the back piece (six o'clock). As you sew the seam, the fastening will not be visible.

STEP 10 Clean off any glue residue from the edges with a piece of eraser and file the edges evenly with a hard nail file.

STEP 11 Burnish the edge as instructed on page 39.

TOTE BAG

IN 1.5 MM THICK LEATHER WITH LACING

MATERIALS

- leather for the front panel, 30 × 40 cm
- leather for the back panel, 30 × 40 cm
- leather for the side panel, 95 × 13 cm
- leather for reinforcing the front and rear panels, 2 pieces of 12.5 × 36.5 cm
- leather for reinforcing the bag's bottom, 1 piece of 30 × 10 cm
- leather for the handles, 4 straps of 85 × 3 cm
- 2 leather cords for the front and rear panels, 140 cm × 5 mm, 1.5 mm thick
- 4 leather cords for the handles, 35 cm × 5 mm, 1.5 mm thick
- cardboard for the patterns

STEP 1 Begin by drawing the patterns directly onto cardboard according to the specified dimensions (image a). This project requires that the patterns be as accurate as possible so that the holes on the front, back and side panels of the bag are in sync with each other. The same pattern can be used for both the front and rear panels, but be sure to turn it upside down when you mark the back panel of the leather in step 8. Draw the rounded corners on the pattern with a pencil compass – I put the points of the compass about 6.5 cm apart and made a 90-degree round angle. Cut out your patterns with a rotary cutter and a ruler for the straight lines and a Stanley knife blade for the round corners – see page 24.

STEP 2 Use a slide rule to mark a line about 8 mm from the edge along the sides and the round corners of the patterns for the front and back panels. Make a similar line along both sides of the pattern for the side panel.

STEP 3 Use the slide rule to mark where you need to make holes in the pattern for the front and back panels by marking dashes that cross the line you made in step 2. The dashes should be spaced 20 mm apart, except for the two top dashes that should be 10 mm from the top edge. In total, make 46 dashes on the pattern for the front and back panels. Make 5 mm holes where the dashes cross the line with a revolving punch.

STEP 4 The holes on the pattern for the side panel must be matched exactly to the holes in the front and rear panels so that the bag can be sewn together. To do this, simply place the pattern for the front and back panel on top of the side panel pattern and mark where the holes are with an awl. Mark one side of the side panel first, then flip the front panel upside down and mark the other side of the side panel. Make 5 mm holes with the revolving punch.

STEP 5 Make a pattern showing where to put the holes in the bag's handles. The pattern should be 12 × 3 cm. Mark a line 1 cm from the edge along both sides of the pattern. Then mark five dashes crossing the lines spaced 20 mm apart (image b). Make a total of ten 5 mm holes with the revolving punch.

STEP 6 Set the strap cutter to 5 mm in width and cut out three straps that are each 140 cm long. Divide one of the straps into four pieces that are each 35 cm long.

STEP 7 Set the strap cutter to a little more than 3 cm in width (include a few extra millimeters on each side so that you can trim off the glue) and cut out four straps that are each 85 cm long.

STEP 8 Mark with a sharp awl on the leather around your patterns and cut out the leather pieces for the front, back and side panels. Use a rotary cutter and a ruler for the straight lines and a Stanley knife blade for the rounded corners. Since the panels will be trimmed after gluing, cut 5 mm above the top edge of the front and rear panels, leaving a margin of a few centimeters on the side panel's short sides. When the leather pieces are cut out, use the patterns to mark where the holes will sit and make the holes in the leather with the revolving punch (image c).

STEP 9 Cut out the reinforcement for the bottom of the bag. Measure the center of the side panel and glue the reinforcing piece according to the instructions on page 28 so that it is 15 cm from the center on each side and evenly spaced from the edges of the side panel. The reinforcement must not cover the holes. Also cut the reinforcement for the bag's front and rear panels and glue them so that they are centered equally from the holes on the sides of the panels. The reinforcement must not cover the holes. When the reinforcement is glued and in place, trim the top edges of the front and rear panels with a rotary cutter and a ruler.

STEP 10 Take the four 85 cm long straps and glue them together two and two, flesh side to flesh side. Set your strap cutter to 3 cm in width and cut away the extra 2 mm margin on each side so that the edges of the straps are completely free of glue residue (image d). Cut off the ends of the straps with a U-shaped punch. An easier alternative for handles is to use two 3 mm thick straps so you will not need to glue and sew them. On the other hand, you won't get the finer hair side on both sides.

⋙⟶ TOOLS

pricking iron
hobby knife or Stanley knife blade
slab for punching/striking
contact adhesive and brush
ruler
needle and thread for saddle stitch
pencil compass
saddler's scratch or compass
strap cutter
revolving punch
rotary knife
round punch, 5 mm
rawhide mallet
slide rule
cutting mat
awl
U-shaped end punch, approx. 3 cm wide

a.

b.

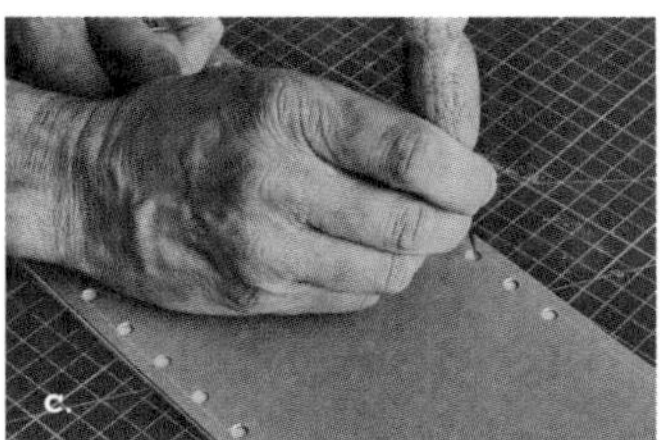
c.

d.

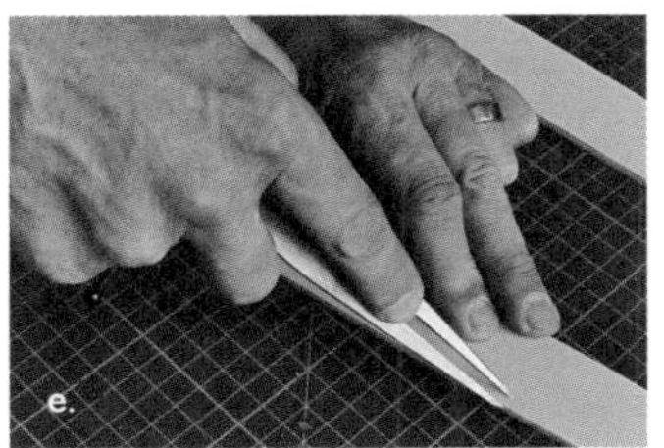
e.

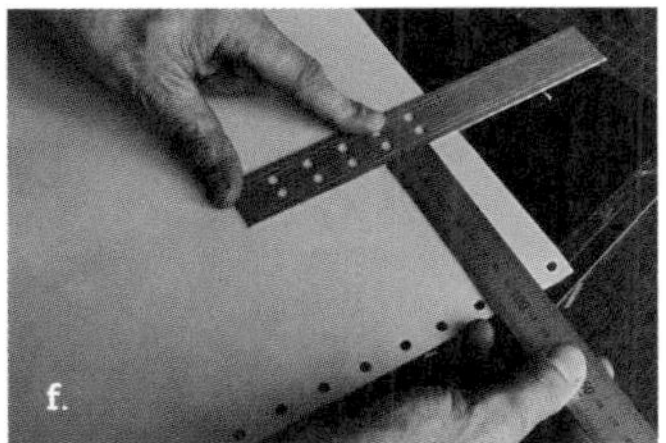
f.

STEP 11 Mark where to put the stitching with a compass 3 mm from the edge along the sides of the handles (image e). Make the stitching holes with the pricking iron along the markings.

STEP 12 Use the pattern you made in step 5 to mark where to put the holes on the handles. You should also use this pattern to mark on the front and back panels where the corresponding holes for the handles will be located. Place the pattern so that the holes are 10 cm from the sides (image f). Make the holes with the revolving punch.

STEP 13 Saddle stitch around the handles according to the instructions on page 35.

STEP 14 Attach the handles to the front and rear panels by threading the four 35 cm long cords through the holes. If you want a knot on the outside of the bag, thread the cords from the outside; make a knot at one end, pull, tighten the cord and tie a knot at the other end. Assemble the front panel and the side panel by threading one of the 140 cm long cords through the holes. Before doing the same to the back panel, cut off the extra margin on the side panel's short ends with a rotary cutter and ruler so that they are level with the front and back panels. Then assemble the rear panel and the side panel. Now the bag is finished.

MESSENGER BAG

IN SOFT 1.5–2 MM THICK LEATHER WITH SHOULDER STRAP

MATERIALS

- leather for the front panel, 30 × 40 cm
- leather for the back panel and top flap, 60 × 40 cm
- leather for the side panel, 115 × 10 cm
- leather for the shoulder strap, 2 pieces 115 cm long and 2 × 40 cm long, twice the width of the buckle you selected
- leather for reinforcement of the top flap, 1 piece, 10 × 40 cm and 2 pieces, 20 × 3 cm
- leather for reinforcement of the front panel's upper edge, 5 × 40 cm
- leather for reinforcement of the side panels and bottom, 2 pieces 8 × 10 cm and 1 piece for the bottom, 25 × 8 cm
- leather for 2 round 35 mm buttons and 2 round 35 mm drawstring
- 8 kangaroo leather-straps for 2 four-stranded round braids, 50 cm × 3 mm, 1 mm thick (braid approx. 30 cm long)
- 1 buckle for the shoulder strap
- cardboard for patterns

STEP 1 Begin by making patterns for all the leather pieces according to the specified dimensions. The front and back panels have rounded corners at the bottom. The side panel is extended approximately 7.5 cm at each end; the extension is folded into the finished bag and serves as two extra inner flaps. If the same soft leather is used for the shoulder strap as for the bag, it should be made double-sided – the straps should be wider than your buckle requires. You will cut the shoulder strap to the correct width after gluing it together. Even buttons made of softer leather need to be double-sided. The drawstring casings should be single-sided and about 2 mm thick. An alternative to making shoulder straps, buttons and drawstrings in the same soft leather as the bag is to use a heavier 3–4 mm thick leather. In this case, the shoulder strap does not need not be double-sided and is cut to the exact width of the buckle. If you want to use the same leather for the drawstrings, you need to thin them down to about 2 mm. You can of course use regular snaps if you do not want to make your own buttons, drawstrings and braids.

STEP 2 Once you have made your patterns and decided on materials and how you want to fasten your bag, put the patterns on your side of leather. Keep in mind that the leather along the spine and closest to the back of the animal (croupon) is more stable and is better suited to the shoulder strap and the front and rear panels. If you want to make your bag high quality and you have enough leather, avoid using the belly part. Once you have placed your patterns, mark around them on the leather with a awl.

STEP 3 Cut out all leather details with a rotary cutter and a long ruler. Don't cut the round corners of the front and back panels; you'll do this only after reinforcing the leather on the top flap and the front.

STEP 4 With a skiving knife, thin the outermost centimeter on one short end of the two 20 × 3 cm pieces of leather (image 1). Reinforce the top flap, which is the upper half of the back panel, by gluing the 10 cm × 40 cm leather piece to the inside of the lower edge of the flap. Follow the instructions for gluing on page 28. Take the two 20 cm × 3 cm leather pieces and place them along the sides of the flap with the short end that was not thinned edge to edge with the 10 cm × 40 cm reinforcement that you glued to the inside of the flap. Use an awl and mark around the leather pieces so you know where to apply the adhesive (image b). Glue the leather pieces together.

STEP 5 Reinforce the front of the bag by gluing the 5 × 40 cm leather piece to the top edge of the front panel (image c). If you want, you can choose to put the eyelets at the bottom of the reinforcement; since the bag lacks inner compartments, the eyelets can be used to attach key chains or wallets. If you choose to use eyelets, leave about 2 cm of the reinforcement unglued.

STEP 6 Cut the round corners of the front and back panels with a hobby knife or Stanley knife blade (image d). I prefer to use the blade for a Stanley knife as it is easier to get the cut 90 degrees to the surface of the leather. I describe how to do this on page 24.

STEP 7 Use the tip of a compass to mark approximately 5 mm from the edge of the front and back panel's hair side. It is within this marking that you will later glue the bag together. Only the sides and the lower edge of the panels should be marked and glued. Also mark 5 mm from the edge along the sides of the side panel. Approximately 92 cm of the side panel length is marked, which corresponds to the dimensions around the front and rear panel sides plus the bottom. To mark, start from the side panel's center point, then mark 46 cm from the center mark and outward so that the marking is centered. When you have made all the markings, carefully file between the marking and the edge of the leather with a nail file or a rough sandpaper to prepare for gluing (image e).

STEP 8 Before gluing the bag, mark where you will put your stitches on the flesh side of the front and back panels. Mark in the same place as you did on the hair side but place the marking slightly farther in: about 7 mm from the edge. Since the flesh side is more difficult to mark with a compass, you should

TOOLS

- oblong punch, approx. 10 mm
- English point end punch
- pricking iron
- slab for punching/striking
- hobby knife or Stanley knife blade
- contact adhesive and brush
- lacing needle to thread in round braids
- long ruler
- nail file or sandpaper
- needle and thread for saddle stitch
- saddler's scratch or compass
- roller
- strap cutter
- revolving punch
- rotary cutter
- round end punch
- gum eraser
- rawhide mallet or hammer
- cutting mat
- skiving knife
- slide rule
- stitching pony
- eyelets and tool for setting

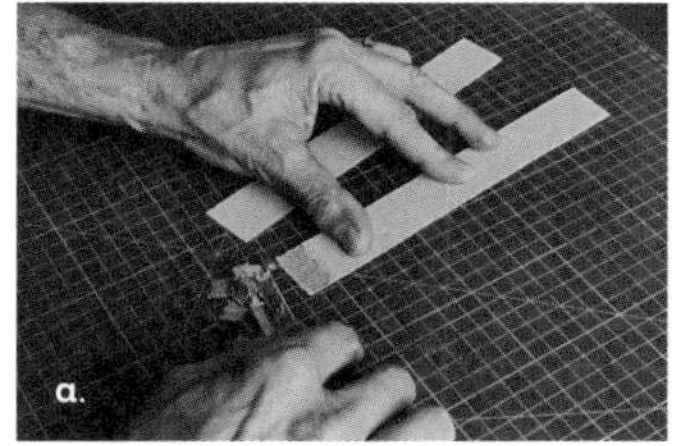
a.

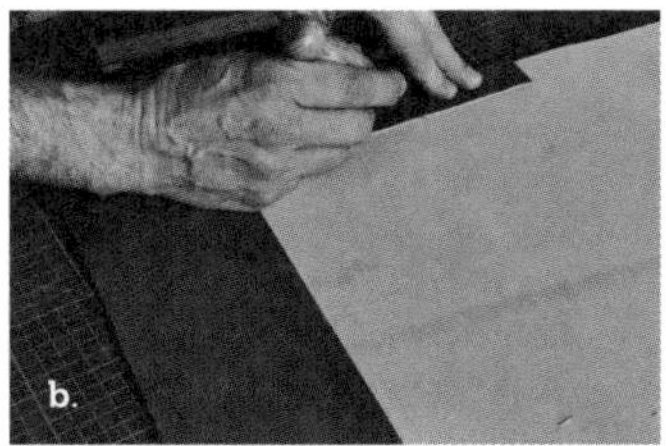
b.

c.

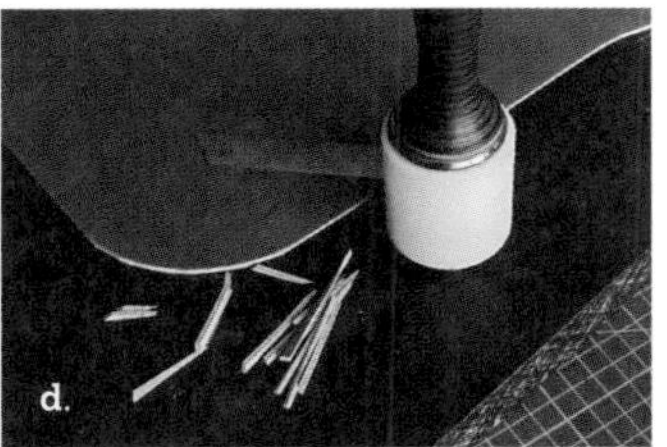
d.

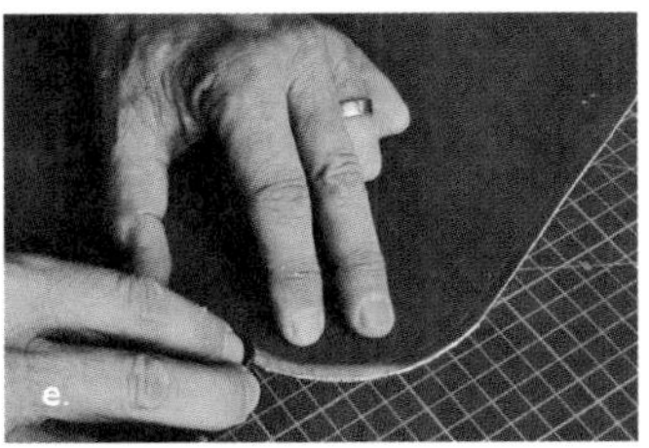
e.

f.

mark it afterward with a pen (image f). Also mark the center of the front and back panels' lower edges, 20 cm from each side. Do the same on the side panels. This makes the joining of the bag's parts easier later.

STEP 9 If you want to make a visible seam around the top flap and along the reinforcement on the front panel, it is easiest to do this before gluing and sewing the bag together. The leather is 4 mm thick, so place the stitching holes about 4 mm from the edge. Mark with a compass around the flap and along the top edge of the front panel, then make stitching holes with a pricking iron along the markings (image g). Sew according to the instructions on page 35 (image h).

STEP 10 The drawstring casings on the front panel can be sewn now or later, when the bag is assembled. The advantage of doing this now is that you have easier access for sewing. The drawstring casings should be sewn approximately 4 cm from the bottom edge of the front panel and about 10 cm from the sides of the front panel – there should be a drawstring casing on each side. The drawstring casings are made of two round 2 mm thick leather pieces, 35 mm in diameter. Marking and stitching holes are made approximately 3 mm from the edge of the drawstrings. Make four 4–5 mm holes whose outer sides form a square in the center of the drawstring casings. Carefully mark with an awl where the drawstring casings should sit on the front panel and sand inside the markings (image q). Apply a narrow line of adhesive around the inside of the marking and around the edge of the drawstring casings (image r). Put them together when the glue is dried. Make the stitching holes in the drawstring casings with a pricking iron and sew a saddle stitch.

STEP 11 Apply adhesive on the hair side of the front, back, and side panels where you previously marked and sanded the surface. While the glue is still tacky, join together the front panel with the side panel. Start by lining up the center marks you made. Then do the same to the back panel and side panel. Be sure to join the parts edge to edge. Press the edges with a roller and then make stitching holes with a pricking iron along the markings you made in step 8. Sew a saddle stitch along the marked edge of the front and rear panels (image i)

STEP 12 Once you have sewn the entire bag, and before turning it inside out, strengthen the edges of the side panel where the shoulder strap will be attached by gluing on the two 8 × 10 cm leather pieces. Reinforce the bottom of the bag by gluing the 8 × 25 cm leather piece (image j). Then turn the bag inside out.

STEP 13 If you chose to use the same soft leather on the shoulder strap as on the bag, you will glue the cut straps flesh side to flesh side. When you are done, you should have a short double-sided shoulder strap and one longer one. Cut the straps to the width that fits your buckle with a strap cutter. Cut off the ends of the straps with an end punch and make a hole for the buckle in the short shoulder strap with an oblong punch (image k). Since the leather is soft and can stretch, sew a saddle stitch along both straps. If you use a thicker strap leather, it is not necessary to sew, but a sewn edge will give it a more finished look. Also make about five round holes in the longer strap with a revolving punch; the holes should be 10 cm from the end and 5 cm apart.

STEP 14 Sew the buckle onto the short shoulder strap: Use an awl to mark two triangles about 5 cm from the end of the strap (image l). Make stitching holes with the pricking iron, insert the buckle in the strap and sew (image m).

STEP 15 To sew the shoulder straps to the upper edges of the side panel, begin by marking the same triangular patterns on the shoulder straps as you did in step 14 (image n). Adjust the seam of the side panel according to the reinforcement you glued to the inside of the top panel. The reinforcement is 10 cm high, and the length of the stitch you mark on the shoulder strap should not be longer. When you have made stitching holes with the pricking iron, first glue the shoulder strap into place, and then sew. Mark out where on the side panels the shoulder straps should sit, then file or sand inside the markings on the side panel and on the back of the shoulder strap. Glue the sanded surfaces and join them when the glue is still tacky. Then mark with a pricking iron again in the holes you made in the shoulder strap. This time the holes are also made through the side panels and reinforcement. Then sew a saddle stitch (image o).

STEP 16 Now all you have left to do is to put the buttons on the bag's flap cover and make the round braids. The buttons

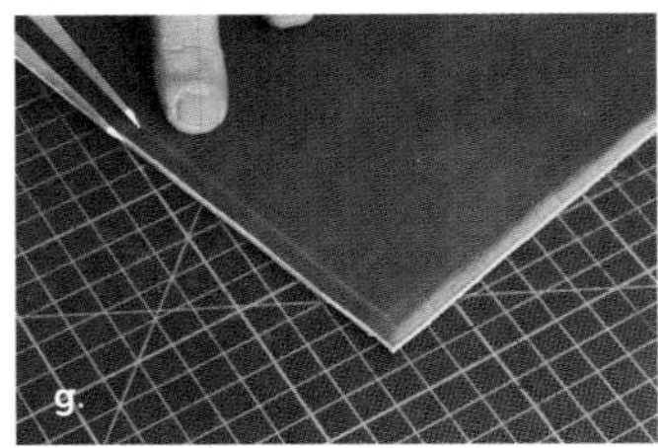
g.

h.

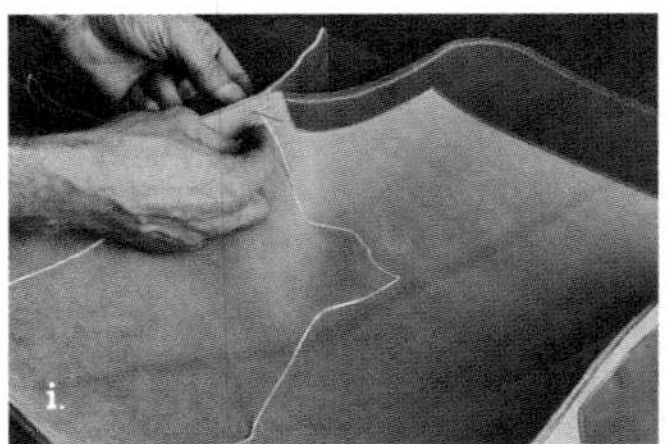
i.

j.

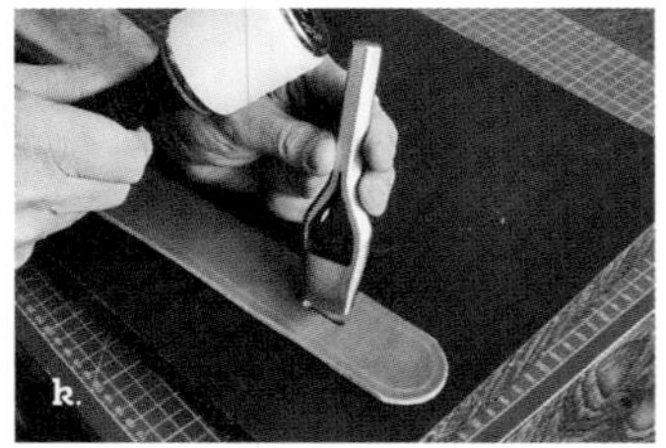
k.

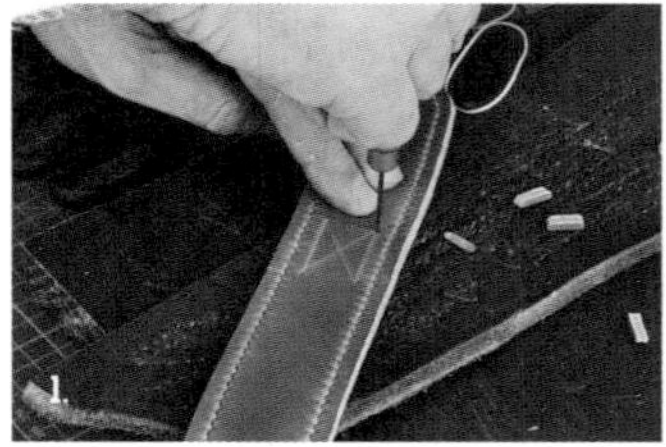
l.

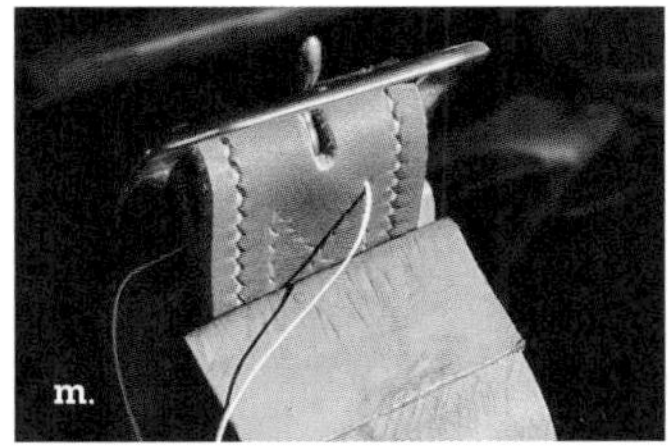
m.

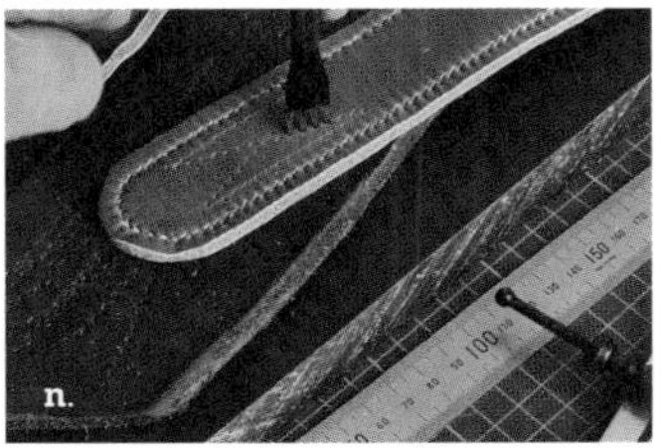
n.

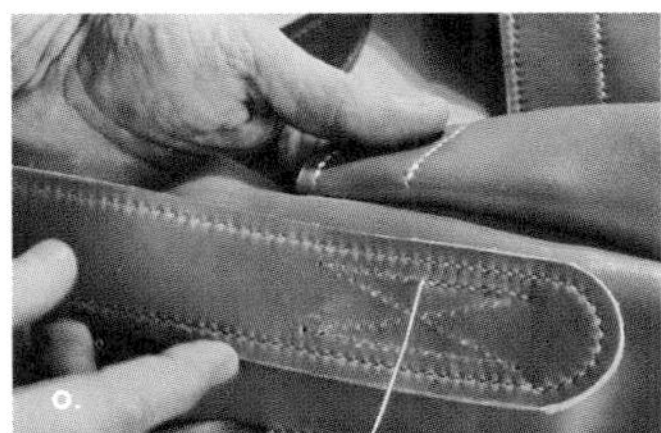
o.

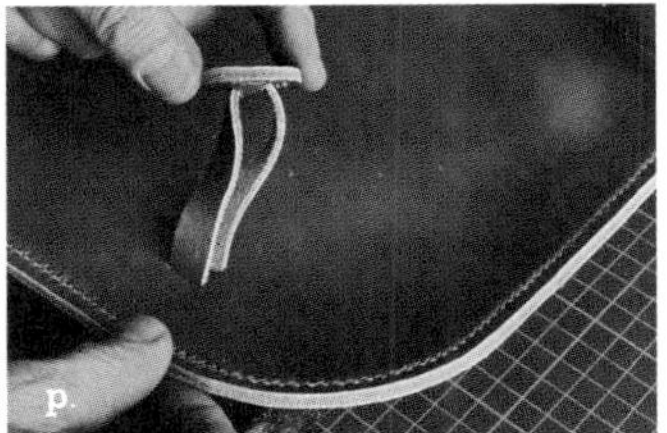
p.

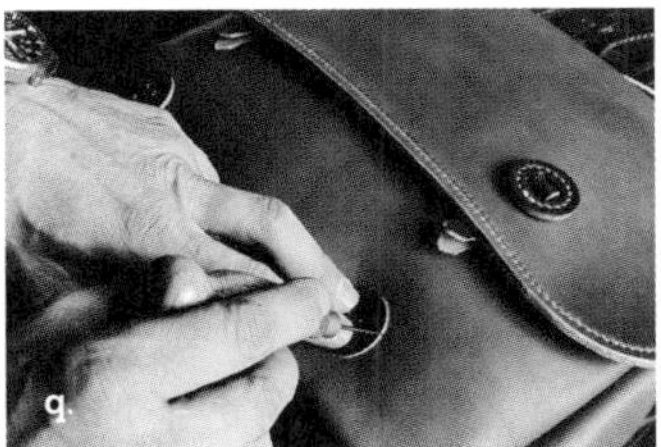
q.

r.

should be the same size as the drawstring casings you made in step 10. Sew around the edge of the buttons and make two parallel holes in the middle with an oblong punch. Place the buttons on the bag's flap cover so that they end up in line with the two drawstring casings you sewed onto the front panel of the bag. Mark on the bag's cover flap with an awl where the buttons should be attached. Then make the same parallel holes in the bag's flap as you did in the buttons with the oblong punch. Thread a leather strap that is as wide as the holes through the button and then through the bag's flap cover (image p). Braid the strap as a hole braid according to the instructions on page 46.

STEP 17 Take the kangaroo leather straps and make two 30 cm long round braids with four strands according to the instructions on page 50, but use a clip or similar instead of a ring when starting the braid. Finish the braid with a Turk's head knot as described on page 53. Tie together the loose end of the braid with a string and attach one of the strands to a lacing needle. Pull the lacing needle through the holes in the drawstring casing. Begin by threading the lacing needle and one of the braid strands through the lower right hole in the drawstring casing and out through the upper right hole. Do the same to the other three strands. When all four strands of the braid have been threaded through, carefully pull the entire braid through the holes. Now do the same on the left side. Finish by making a Turk's head knot on the other end of the braid that you tied with a string. Now the bag is finished!

MORE INFO

GLOSSARY

It may be helpful or interesting to know some Swedish-English technical terms when searching the web for tools or further information on Swedish-style leatherworking techniques.

Swedish	English
Bivax	Beeswax
Exacto-kniv	X-Acto knife
Falsben	Bone folder
Gaffelmejsel för handsömnad	Pricking iron
Gaffelmejsel för laskning	Lacing awl or thonging chisel
Gropjärn, ställbar	Adjustable gouge
Hammare	Mallet or hammer
Huggjärn	End punch
Huggpipa, avlång	Oblong punch
Huggpipa, rund	Round punch
Huggplatta	Cutting board
Kantpolerare	Burnisher or edge slicker
Kantskärare	Edger
Klämmor	Bulldog clips
Kontaktlim	Rubber solution
Lasknål	Lacing needle
Linjal	Ruler
Läderfett	Leather conditioner, saddle soap
Markeringshjul	Stitching wheel
Narvsvärta	Leather dye
Nitjärn	Stud setter die, rivet setter die or snap setter die
Passare med dubbel spets	Saddler's scratch, gauge compass
Passare med blyertspets	Gauge compass
Plattång	Flat nose pliers, lacing pliers
Polerpasta eller dragantgummi	Tragacanth burnishing gum
Remskärare	Strap cutter, plough gauge or draw gauge
Revolverhålslag	Revolving punch
Ross eller systol	Saddler's stitching horse
Rullkniv	Rotary knife
Rågummi	Crepe rubber
Räffeljärn	Creaser
Räffelträ	Wood creaser
Sadelmakarklämma eller syklov	Stitching pony
Sadelmakarnål	Harness needles
Sandpapper	Sandpaper
Skjutmått	Slide rule
Skärflingshyvel	Skiver
Skärflingskniv	Skiving knife
Skärmatta	Cutting mat
Stanley-kniv	Stanley knife
Syl	Awl
Sylskaft till rundsyl	Awl handle for round blade
Sylskaft till skärsyl	Awl handle for diamond blade
Syrännejärn	Stitching groover
Vaxad lintråd	Waxed linen thread
Vaxad syntettråd	Waxed synthetic thread
Vaxpenna	Marking pen

SUPPLIERS

LEATHER

ALCE Leather
Åsbyvägen 10
782 30 Malung
Sweden
www.malgarv.se

Hermann Oak Leather Company
4050 North First Street
St Louis, Missouri 63147
www.hermannoakleather.com

Horween Leather Company
2015 North Elston Ave
Chicago, Illinois 60614
www.horween.com

MG Leather
Gustafsson Skinn & Läder
Solvarvsgatan 4
507 40 Borås
Sweden
www.mgleather.se

Tärnsjö
Garverivägen 6
740 45 Tärnsjö
Sweden
www.tarnsjogarveri.com

TOOLS

Barry King Tools
1751 Terra Ave
Sheridan, Wyoming 82801
www.barrykingtools.com

Fine Leatherworking
1569 Solano Ave. #625
Berkeley, California 94707
www.fineleatherworking.com

Goods Japan
www.goodsjapan.jp

Laederiet Aps
Mossövej 11
8240 Risskov
Denmark
www.laederiet.dk

Osborne Leather Tools
125 Jersey Street
Harrison, New Jersey 07029
www.osborneleathertools.com

Sadelmakarna AB
Sunnanå 30
186 95 Vallentuna
Sweden
www.sadelmakarna.com

Slöjd-Detaljer
Mäster Samuelsgatan 56
111 21 Stockholm
Sweden
www.slojd-detaljer.se

Tandy Leather
Many locations worldwide
www.tandyleatherfactory.com

Vergez Blanchard
La Taillanderie BP9
27610 Romilly-sur-Andelle
France
www.vergez-blanchard.fr

BUCKLES, FASTENERS AND FITTINGS

BuckleGuy
15 Graf Rd.
Newburyport, Massachusetts 01950
www.buckleguy.com

Sadelmakarna AB
Sunnanå 30
186 95 Vallentuna
Sweden
www.sadelmakarna.com

»—→ REFERENCES

Encyclopedia of Rawhide and Leather Braiding
Grant, Bruce, 1972
Cornell Maritime Press

Leather Braiding
Grant, Bruce, 1997
Cornell Maritime Press

The Art of Hand Sewing Leather
Stohlman, Al, 1977
Tandy Leather Co.

The Leatherworking Handbook
Valerie, Michael, 2006
Cassell

Motorcycle Accessory Pattern Pack
Tandy Leather Co.

»—→ THANK YOU!

First of all, I would like to thank my beautiful wife for all her inspiration and encouragement, and for her great patience when our kitchen was transformed into one big workshop.

I would also like to thank Douglas and Hampus at Unionville. Without their eye for good handicraft, I would not have resumed my work with leather.

Last but not least, I would like to thank Magnus Nyström and Carl Johan Dahlin at Nyström Stockholm for their always-friendly assistance, their good advice and many helpful tips.

»—→ INDEX

English Edition

2332 Fourth Street, Suite E
Berkeley, CA 94710
Typesetting Weiß-Freiburg GmbH –
Graphik & Buchgestaltung
Translation by Dolmetscher - und
Übersetzer Service Gerhard Herzet

ISBN: 978-1-58423-661-0

www.gingkopress.com

Original title: Lone Wolf läderarbete First
Published by Natur & Kultur, Sweden
Photos Calle Stoltz
Illustration Kristin Lidström
Text Jonas Cramby
Editor Russell Walls

Printed in China